VEGETARIAN COOKING

Edited by
Carole Handslip

Contents

This edition first published 1980 by
Octopus Books Limited
59 Grosvenor Street, London W1

© 1980 Octopus Books Limited

ISBN 0 7064 1284 2

Produced and printed in Hong Kong by
Mandarin Publishers Limited
22a Westlands Road, Quarry Bay

Frontispiece: FRESH VEGETABLES AND FRUIT

Weights and Measures

All measurements in this book are given in Metric, Imperial and American.

Measurements in weight in the Imperial and American system are the same. Liquid measurements are different, and the following table shows the equivalents:

Liquid measurements

1 Imperial pint	20 fluid ounces
1 American pint	16 fluid ounces
1 American cup	8 fluid ounces

Level spoon measurements are used in all recipes.

Spoon measurements

1 tablespoon	15 ml
1 teaspoon	5 ml

When preparing the recipes in this book, only follow one set of measures – they are not interchangeable.

INTRODUCTION

Today there is a growing interest in organically grown vegetables and whole foods, with the result that more and more people are discovering that the range of vegetarian dishes can be both imaginative and full of variety.

The aim of this book is to inspire all adventurous cooks – vegetarians and non-vegetarians alike – to experiment and try out new ingredients. A vegetarian diet can provide all the essential nutrients we require for good health, including fats, essential minerals and vitamins. Meat is considered by many people to be a vital part of a balanced diet, and it is essential that strict vegetarians plan their diet carefully to ensure that they obtain an adequate supply of amino acids and iron. It is important, therefore, that all ingredients are fresh, wholesome and in perfect condition.

It is a good idea to seek out reliable suppliers where you can be sure of finding natural, unprocessed ingredients. Shopping in specialist stores is often more enjoyable and usually well worth the extra expense; the flavour in the food is just one of the bonuses.

In these weight- and calorie-conscious times, salads are becoming increasingly popular. Raw vegetables are especially good for you as they provide essential roughage and none of the nutrients are lost during cooking. Some vegetables, such as courgettes (zucchini), cauliflower and leeks, are more appetizing if first blanched in boiling water, then drained and rinsed in cold water while still crisp.

No salad is complete without a homemade dressing, and there are endless possibilities for combining ingredients like herb oils, fruit juices, mustards and spices. For a light creamy dressing, try adding fresh herbs and seasonings to natural yogurt.

To add interest to a vegetarian meal, think carefully about the ways in which you can vary the flavours and contrast textures. A thick bean soup, served with a crisp fresh salad and crusty wholewheat bread, for example, can make a complete and satisfying meal. Alternatively, serve a variety of individual vegetable dishes with different sauces as the main course, keeping in mind the way in which Chinese and Indian meals are presented. Make the most of herbs, freshly picked from the garden or from a pot on the kitchen windowsill, and discover how to season foods with blends of aromatic spices. It is these different and subtle flavours which transform everyday ingredients into delicious and memorable meals.

It is hoped that everyone, whether a committed vegetarian or not, will enjoy planning, preparing and sampling this collection of exciting vegetarian dishes.

YOGURT WHOLEWHEAT SCONES *(page 88)*

SOUPS

Lentil Soup

METRIC/IMPERIAL	AMERICAN
900 ml/1 ½ pints water	3¾ cups water
1 rounded teaspoon yeast extract	1 rounded teaspoon brewer's yeast
100 g/4 oz lentils	½ cup lentils
1 large carrot, chopped	1 large carrot, chopped
1 large onion, chopped	1 large onion, chopped
1 tablespoon tomato purée	1 tablespoon tomato paste
1 tablespoon wholewheat flour	1 tablespoon wholewheat flour
300 ml/½ pint milk	1¼ cups milk
salt	salt
freshly ground black pepper	freshly ground black pepper
2 slices wholewheat bread to serve	2 slices wholewheat bread to serve

Heat a little of the water in a small pan, add the yeast extract (brewer's yeast) and stir until dissolved. Place the remaining water in a large saucepan, add the dissolved yeast extract (brewer's yeast) and lentils, cover the pan and bring to the boil. Remove from the heat and leave to stand overnight.

Bring the lentils back to the boil, then add the carrot, onion and tomato purée (paste). Simmer, covered, for 1 hour.

Blend the flour with a little of the milk. Stir in the rest of the milk, then stir into the soup. Bring to the boil, stirring, then simmer for 2 minutes until thickened. Season to taste with salt and pepper.

Toast the bread, cut into small squares and serve with the soup.
Serves 4

Bean and Carrot Soup

METRIC/IMPERIAL	AMERICAN
50 g/2 oz butter	1/4 cup butter
500 g/1 lb carrots, sliced	3 cups sliced carrot
1 large potato, diced	1 large potato, diced
1 medium onion, chopped	1 medium onion, chopped
900 ml/1 1/2 pints water	3 1/4 cups water
1 tablespoon tomato purée	1 tablespoon tomato paste
good pinch of ground coriander	good pinch of ground coriander
salt	salt
freshly ground black pepper	freshly ground black pepper
1 × 425 g/15 oz can kidney beans, drained	1 × 15 oz can kidney beans, drained
chopped parsley to garnish	chopped parsley to garnish

Melt the butter in a saucepan, add the vegetables and cook, stirring, for 5 minutes. Add the water, tomato purée (paste), coriander and salt and pepper to taste. Bring to the boil, then lower the heat, cover and simmer for 45 minutes.

Stir in the kidney beans and reheat gently. Pour into individual soup bowls, garnish with parsley and serve at once.
Serves 4

Cream of Spinach Soup

METRIC/IMPERIAL	AMERICAN
50 g/2 oz butter	1/4 cup butter
1 medium onion, finely chopped	1 medium onion, finely chopped
25 g/1 oz wholewheat flour	1/4 cup wholewheat flour
600 ml/1 pint milk	2 1/2 cups milk
1 × 227 g/8 oz packet frozen chopped spinach, thawed	1 × 1/2 lb package frozen chopped spinach, thawed
300 ml/1/2 pint stock	1 1/4 cups stock
salt	salt
freshly ground black pepper	freshly ground black pepper
grated nutmeg	grated nutmeg
3 tablespoons double cream	3 tablespoons heavy cream

Melt the butter in a saucepan. Add the onion and cook gently for 5 minutes. Stir in the flour and cook for 2 minutes. Heat the milk in a separate pan, then add to the onion with the spinach, stock, and salt, pepper and nutmeg to taste. Simmer for 20 minutes.

Work the soup in an electric blender or rub through a coarse sieve until smooth. Reheat gently and stir in the cream. Check the seasoning and serve.
Serves 4

Thick Bean and Vegetable Soup

METRIC/IMPERIAL	AMERICAN
225 g/8 oz haricot beans, soaked overnight	*1 cup plus 2 tablespoons navy beans, soaked overnight*
3 tablespoons olive oil	*3 tablespoons olive oil*
1 onion, chopped	*1 onion, chopped*
1 garlic clove, crushed	*1 garlic clove, crushed*
1 stick celery, chopped	*1 celery stalk, chopped*
2 leeks, thinly sliced	*2 leeks, thinly sliced*
500 g/1 lb green cabbage, finely shredded	*6 cups finely shredded green cabbage*
1 sprig each of thyme and rosemary, tied together	*1 sprig each of thyme and rosemary, tied together*
1 tablespoon tomato purée	*1 tablespoon tomato paste*
sea salt	*coarse salt*
freshly ground black pepper	*freshly ground black pepper*
2 tablespoons chopped parsley	*2 tablespoons chopped parsley*
croûtons to serve	*croûtons to serve*

Drain the beans and place in a saucepan. Add 1.75 litres/3 pints/ 7½ cups cold water, bring to the boil, cover and simmer for about 2 hours or until tender.

Meanwhile, heat the oil in a large saucepan, add the onion, garlic and celery and fry gently for 10 minutes, stirring frequently. Add the leeks, cabbage and herbs and stir for 3 to 4 minutes.

Drain the beans and add the cooking liquor to the vegetables, together with the tomato purée (paste) and salt and pepper to taste. Bring to the boil and simmer for about 30 minutes. Add the beans, with more water as necessary, and continue simmering until all the vegetables are tender. Remove the herbs and check the seasoning. Stir in the parsley and serve immediately. Hand the croûtons separately.

Serves 6 to 8

Chestnut Soup

METRIC/IMPERIAL	AMERICAN
750 g/1 ½ lb fresh chestnuts	5 cups fresh chestnuts
25 g/1 oz butter or margarine	2 tablespoons butter or margarine
1 onion, sliced	1 onion, sliced
1 carrot, sliced	1 carrot, sliced
1 celery stick, chopped	1 celery stalk, chopped
900 ml/1 ½ pints stock	3 ¾ cups stock
sea salt	coarse salt
freshly ground black pepper	freshly ground black pepper
150 ml/¼ pint single cream	⅔ cup light cream

Place the chestnuts in a pan and cover with water. Bring to the boil and simmer for 10 minutes. Cool slightly, then peel them.

Heat the butter or margarine in a pan, add the vegetables and cook for 5 minutes. Add the stock, chestnuts, and salt and pepper to taste. Bring to the boil and simmer for 30 to 40 minutes, until the nuts are tender. Rub through a sieve or work in an electric blender until smooth and return to the pan. Add the cream and heat gently. Pour into a warmed soup tureen.
Serves 4 to 6

Summer Tomato Soup

METRIC/IMPERIAL	AMERICAN
500 g/1 lb tomatoes, skinned, seeded and chopped	2 cups skinned, seeded and chopped tomatoes
100 g/4 oz cucumber, peeled and chopped	1 cup peeled and diced cucumber
1 garlic clove, crushed	1 garlic clove, minced
pinch of cayenne pepper	pinch of cayenne pepper
pinch of salt	pinch of salt
2 teaspoons Worcestershire sauce	2 teaspoons Worcestershire sauce
1 medium green pepper, cored, seeded and chopped	1 medium green pepper, cored, seeded and chopped
1 × 141 g/5 oz carton natural yogurt	⅔ cup unflavored yogurt
chopped parsley to garnish	chopped parsley to garnish

Put all the ingredients, except half of the green pepper and the yogurt, in an electric blender and work until smooth. Chill well. Stir in the remaining green pepper and the yogurt and sprinkle with parsley before serving.
Serves 4

Potato and Leek Soup

METRIC/IMPERIAL	AMERICAN
50 g/2 oz butter	1/4 cup butter
500 g/1 lb leeks, sliced	1 lb leeks, sliced
225 g/8 oz potatoes, sliced	1/2 lb potatoes, sliced
1 parsnip, sliced	1 parsnip, sliced
600 ml/1 pint stock	2 1/2 cups stock
salt	salt
freshly ground black pepper	freshly ground black pepper
150 ml/1/4 pint single cream	2/3 cup light cream
snipped chives to garnish	snipped chives to garnish

Melt the butter in a large frying pan (skillet); add the vegetables and fry gently until soft. Add the stock, and salt and pepper to taste. Bring to the boil, then cover and simmer for 1 hour or until all the vegetables are really tender.

Cool slightly, then place in an electric blender and work until smooth. Return to the pan, stir in the cream and heat through, but do not allow to boil. Garnish with chives to serve.

Serves 4

Chilled Cucumber Soup

METRIC/IMPERIAL	AMERICAN
50 g/2 oz butter	1/4 cup butter
1 medium onion, finely chopped	1 medium onion, finely chopped
1 large cucumber, diced	1 large cucumber, diced
25 g/1 oz plain flour	1/4 cup all-purpose flour
salt	salt
freshly ground black pepper	freshly ground black pepper
600 ml/1 pint stock	2 1/2 cups stock
300 ml/1/2 pint milk	1 1/4 cups milk
5 tablespoons soured cream	1/3 cup sour cream
a few cucumber slices to garnish	a few cucumber slices to garnish

Melt the butter in a saucepan. Add the onion and cucumber and cook gently for 10 minutes, stirring. Add the flour and cook for 2 minutes. Season to taste with salt and pepper, then stir in the stock and milk. Bring to the boil, then simmer for 15 minutes.

Place in an electric blender and work until smooth. Chill well, then stir in the soured cream. Garnish with cucumber slices to serve.

Serves 4

Gazpacho

METRIC/IMPERIAL

750 g/1½ lb ripe tomatoes, skinned
  and chopped
2 medium onions, chopped
2 garlic cloves, chopped
1 green pepper, cored, seeded and
  diced
½ medium cucumber, diced
2 tablespoons lemon juice
2 tablespoons olive oil
salt
freshly ground black pepper
iced water

AMERICAN

3 cups skinned and chopped
  tomatoes
2 medium onions, chopped
2 garlic cloves, chopped
1 green pepper, cored, seeded and
  diced
½ medium cucumber, diced
2 tablespoons lemon juice
2 tablespoons olive oil
salt
freshly ground black pepper
iced water

Put the tomatoes, one of the onions and the garlic into a saucepan.
Simmer until the tomatoes have softened slightly. Sieve, or work in
an electric blender, then strain.

Add half the pepper, half the cucumber, the lemon juice, oil, salt
and pepper to taste, and enough iced water to give the consistency of
a moderately thick soup. Chill thoroughly until required.

Place the reserved vegetables in separate dishes, cover and chill.
Serve with the soup.
Serves 4 to 6

Chilled Beetroot (Beet) Soup

METRIC/IMPERIAL

2 beetroot, cooked and roughly
  chopped
600 ml/1 pint stock
2 tablespoons white wine vinegar
grated zest and juice of 1 large
  orange
sea salt
freshly ground black pepper
300 ml/½ pint single cream

AMERICAN

2 beet, cooked and roughly chopped
2½ cups stock
2 tablespoons white wine vinegar
grated zest and juice of 1 large
  orange
coarse salt
freshly ground black pepper
1¼ cups light cream

Place the beetroot (beet), stock, vinegar, orange zest and juice, and
salt and pepper to taste in an electric blender and work until smooth.
Stir in the cream and chill well.
Serves 4

FIRST COURSES

Stuffed Mushrooms

METRIC/IMPERIAL	AMERICAN
12 large mushrooms	12 large mushrooms
3 tablespoons olive oil	3 tablespoons olive oil
1 garlic clove, chopped	1 garlic clove, chopped
3 shallots, chopped	3 shallots, chopped
25 g/1 oz wholewheat breadcrumbs	½ cup wholewheat breadcrumbs
50 g/2 oz grated Parmesan cheese	½ cup grated Parmesan cheese
1 teaspoon snipped chives	1 teaspoon snipped chives
2 teaspoons chopped parsley	2 teaspoons chopped parsley
salt	salt
freshly ground black pepper	freshly ground black pepper
25 g/1 oz butter	2 tablespoons butter

Wipe the mushrooms with a damp cloth. Remove the stalks and chop them finely.

Heat the oil in a frying pan (skillet), add the garlic, shallots and mushroom stalks and cook, stirring, for about 5 minutes. Remove from the heat, add the remaining ingredients, except the butter, and mix well.

Arrange the mushroom caps in a greased flameproof dish, fill with the mixture and dot with the butter. Place under a preheated medium grill (broiler) for 5 minutes, until golden. Serve at once.
Serves 4

18

Cheese-stuffed Tomatoes

METRIC/IMPERIAL
4 large tomatoes
3 dessert apples, peeled, cored and
* chopped*
8 stuffed green olives, sliced
2 tablespoons French dressing (see
* page 79)*
1 stick celery, sliced
50 g/2 oz Danish blue cheese, diced
4 tablespoons mayonnaise (see page
* 72)*
chopped parsley to garnish
4 lettuce leaves to serve

AMERICAN
4 large tomatoes
3 dessert apples, peeled, cored and
* chopped*
8 pimiento-stuffed green olives,
* sliced*
2 tablespoons French dressing (see
* page 79)*
1 celery stalk, sliced
½ cup diced Danish blue cheese
¼ cup mayonnaise (see page 72)
chopped parsley to garnish
4 lettuce leaves to serve

Cut the tops off the tomatoes, scoop out the flesh and leave the tomatoes upside down to drain. Mix together the apple, olives, dressing, celery and cheese. Fill the tomatoes with this mixture and spoon over the mayonnaise. Sprinkle with chopped parsley and serve on a lettuce leaf.
Serves 4

Potted Mushrooms

METRIC/IMPERIAL
75 g/3 oz butter
500 g/1 lb mushrooms, chopped
1 teaspoon chopped thyme
1 teaspoon chopped parsley
salt
freshly ground black pepper

AMERICAN
⅓ cup butter
4 cups chopped mushrooms
1 teaspoon chopped thyme
1 teaspoon chopped parsley
salt
freshly ground black pepper

Melt 25 g/1 oz/2 tablespoons of the butter in a saucepan. Add the mushrooms, herbs, and salt and pepper to taste. Cover and cook very slowly for 10 minutes. Using a slotted spoon, lift out the mushrooms and chop very finely.

Meanwhile, boil the liquid in the pan until reduced to 2 to 3 tablespoons. Mix in the mushrooms and check the seasoning.

Pack tightly into 4 ramekin dishes, smooth the top and chill well.

Melt the remaining butter, skim the surface and pour into each dish to cover the mushrooms completely. Return to the refrigerator to set. Serve with wholewheat rolls.
Serves 4

Crispy Fried Vegetables with Garlic Mayonnaise

METRIC/IMPERIAL
500 g/1 lb vegetables (see below)
Batter:
2 eggs, separated
300 ml/½ pint pale ale
25 g/1 oz butter, melted
175 g/6 oz plain flour
1 teaspoon dry mustard
salt
freshly ground black pepper
oil for deep frying
Garlic mayonnaise:
150 ml/¼ pint mayonnaise (see
  page 72)
2 tablespoons double cream
2 garlic cloves, crushed
1 tablespoon dried mixed herbs

AMERICAN
1 lb vegetables (see below)
Batter:
2 eggs, separated
1¼ cups beer
2 tablespoons butter, melted
1½ cups all-purpose flour
1 teaspoon dry mustard
salt
freshly ground black pepper
oil for deep frying
Garlic mayonnaise:
⅔ cup mayonnaise (see page 72)
2 tablespoons heavy cream
2 garlic cloves, crushed
1 tablespoon dried mixed herbs

A variety of vegetables can be used for this recipe, including aubergine (eggplant), celeriac, courgettes (zucchini), cauliflower florets, Jerusalem artichokes, fennel, mushrooms, parsnip, etc. Use courgettes (zucchini) and mushrooms raw; steam or boil the others until half cooked. Cut into pieces the size of medium mushrooms.

To make the batter: mix the egg yolks and beer together, add the butter and beat until smooth. Sift the flour and mustard into a bowl and gradually beat in the egg mixture, adding salt and pepper to taste. Whisk the egg whites until very stiff, then fold into the batter. Mix the mayonnaise ingredients together and place in a serving dish.

Dip each piece of vegetable into the batter, making sure it is completely coated, and fry in hot oil until golden brown and crisp. Drain on kitchen paper towels and serve at once, with the mayonnaise served separately as a dip.
Serves 4 to 6

Stuffed Avocado

METRIC/IMPERIAL	AMERICAN
1 × 326 g/11½ oz can sweetcorn, drained	1 × 11½ oz can kernel corn, drained
225 g/8 oz cottage cheese	1 × ½ lb container ricotta cheese
2 tablespoons snipped chives	2 tablespoons snipped chives
salt	salt
freshly ground black pepper	freshly ground black pepper
4 avocados	4 avocados
squeeze of lemon juice	squeeze of lemon juice
lettuce leaves to serve	lettuce leaves to serve

Mix together the corn, cheese and chives. Season to taste with salt and pepper. Halve the pears, discard the stones (pits) and brush with lemon juice. Divide the mixture between the pears, and serve on a bed of lettuce.
Serves 8

Peperonata

METRIC/IMPERIAL	AMERICAN
150 ml/¼ pint olive oil	⅔ cup olive oil
1 kg/2 lb red and green peppers, cored, seeded and sliced	2 lb red and green peppers, cored, seeded and sliced
1 large onion, sliced	1 large onion, sliced
500 g/1 lb tomatoes, skinned and sliced	1 lb tomatoes, skinned and sliced
2 garlic cloves, chopped	2 garlic cloves, minced
salt	salt
freshly ground black pepper	freshly ground black pepper

Heat the oil in a large pan, add the vegetables and garlic, cover and cook gently for 15 minutes. Add salt and pepper to taste, and cook for a further 10 minutes. Serve hot or cold, with French bread.
Serves 4 to 6

Celeriac Rémoulade

METRIC/IMPERIAL
1 head celeriac, cut into julienne
  strips
1 tablespoon white wine vinegar
salt
6 tablespoons mayonnaise (see page
  72)
1½ tablespoons French mustard
1½ tablespoons lemon juice

AMERICAN
1 head celeriac (celery root), cut
  into strips
1 tablespoon white wine vinegar
salt
6 tablespoons mayonnaise (see page
  72)
1½ tablespoons French mustard
1½ tablespoons lemon juice

Put the celeriac in a bowl, cover with water and add the vinegar and
a little salt to prevent discoloration. Allow to stand for 15 minutes
then drain.

Blanch the celeriac in boiling water for 15 seconds. Drain, rinse
under cold water, then drain well and leave to cool. Place in a serving
dish. Combine the mayonnaise, mustard and lemon juice, pour over
the celeriac and toss well to coat. Chill well before serving.
Serves 4

Butter Bean (Wax Bean) Vinaigrette

METRIC/IMPERIAL
175 g/6 oz butter beans, soaked
  overnight
salt
3 tablespoons French dressing
  (see page 79)
1 small onion, finely chopped
1 tablespoon chopped parsley

AMERICAN
1 cup wax beans, soaked overnight
salt
3 tablespoons French dressing
  (see page 79)
1 small onion, finely chopped
1 tablespoon chopped parsley

Drain the beans, place in a pan and cover with fresh water. Bring to
the boil, cover and simmer for 1½ to 2 hours, adding salt to taste
towards the end of cooking.

Drain the beans and add the remaining ingredients while still
warm. Toss together well to coat and leave to cool.
Serves 4 to 5

Tomatoes with Yogurt

METRIC/IMPERIAL	AMERICAN
50 g/2 oz butter	¼ cup butter
500 g/1 lb tomatoes, skinned and chopped	2 cups skinned and chopped tomatoes
pinch of sugar	pinch of sugar
2 × 141 g/5 oz cartons natural yogurt	1¼ cups unflavored yogurt
sea salt	coarse salt
freshly ground black pepper	freshly ground black pepper
2 tablespoons chopped basil	2 tablespoons chopped basil
25 g/1 oz pine kernels	¼ cup pine nuts (pignoli)
1 pitta bread to garnish	1 Euphrates bread to garnish

Melt the butter in a shallow pan, add the tomatoes and cook gently for a few minutes, until just softened. Remove the pan from the heat. Add the sugar, yogurt and salt and pepper to taste.

Stir in the basil, then pour into a shallow serving dish and scatter the pine kernels (nuts) over the top. Serve warm with pitta (Euphrates) bread.

Serves 4

Pear and Grape Salad

METRIC/IMPERIAL	AMERICAN
4 ripe pears, peeled, halved and cored	4 ripe pears, peeled, halved and cored
175 g/6 oz cream cheese	¾ cup cream cheese
3 tablespoons mayonnaise (see page 72)	3 tablespoons mayonnaise (see page 72)
salt	salt
freshly ground black pepper	freshly ground black pepper
paprika	paprika
225 g/8 oz green grapes, skinned, pipped and halved	2 cups white grapes, skinned, seeded and halved
watercress to garnish	watercress to garnish

Arrange the pears, cut side down, on a serving dish. Mix together the cream cheese and mayonnaise and add salt and pepper to taste. Spread the mixture all over the pears, then press the grapes in firmly. Garnish with watercress.

Serves 4

Arabian Aubergine (Eggplant)

METRIC/IMPERIAL
2 small aubergines, peeled and
  cubed
salt
4 tablespoons olive oil
1 garlic clove, crushed
½ small onion, minced
juice of 1 lemon
2 tablespoons chopped parsley
150 ml/¼ pint soured cream
mint sprigs to garnish

AMERICAN
2 small eggplants, peeled and cubed
salt
¼ cup olive oil
1 garlic clove, minced
½ small onion, minced
juice of 1 lemon
2 tablespoons chopped parsley
⅔ cup sour cream
mint sprigs to garnish

Sprinkle the aubergine (eggplant) with salt and leave to drain for
30 minutes. Rinse and pat dry on kitchen paper towels.

Heat the oil in a frying pan (skillet). Add the aubergine (eggplant)
and sauté for 6 minutes, turning occasionally. Place in a serving dish
and add the remaining ingredients. Mix well then place in the
refrigerator for 3 hours. Garnish with mint and serve with
wholewheat bread.
Serves 4

Aubergine (Eggplant) Pâté

METRIC/IMPERIAL
3 large aubergines
1 garlic clove, crushed
1 tablespoon minced onion
2 tablespoons olive oil
1 tablespoon lemon juice
salt
freshly ground black pepper
1 tablespoon chopped parsley to
  garnish

AMERICAN
3 large eggplants
1 garlic clove, minced
1 tablespoon minced onion
2 tablespoons olive oil
1 tablespoon lemon juice
salt
freshly ground black pepper
1 tablespoon chopped parsley to
  garnish

Place the aubergines (eggplants) in a baking dish, place in a preheated
moderate oven (180°C/350°F, Gas Mark 4) and cook for 1 hour.

Cut the aubergines (eggplants) in half and scoop out the flesh.
Place in an electric blender with the remaining ingredients, adding
salt and pepper to taste, and work until smooth. Spoon into 6
individual dishes and chill until firm.

Sprinkle with chopped parsley and serve with toast.
Serves 6

Mushroom and Egg Ramekins

METRIC/IMPERIAL
175 g/6 oz small button mushrooms
1 garlic clove, crushed
150 ml/¼ pint stock
salt
freshly ground black pepper
4 eggs
1 tablespoon chopped parsley

AMERICAN
1½ cups small mushrooms
1 garlic clove, crushed
⅔ cup white stock
salt
freshly ground black pepper
4 eggs
1 tablespoon chopped parsley

Place the mushrooms, garlic and stock in a pan. Simmer uncovered, adding salt and pepper to taste.

Meanwhile, poach the eggs and place in 4 ramekin dishes.

Stir the parsley into the mushroom mixture, pour over the eggs and serve immediately.

Serves 4

Devilled Cottage Eggs

METRIC/IMPERIAL
4 hard-boiled eggs
¼ teaspoon dry mustard
2 teaspoons vinegar
1 tablespoon chutney
225 g/8 oz cottage cheese
¼ teaspoon salt
pinch of cayenne pepper or paprika
1 teaspoon chopped chives
To garnish:
parsley sprigs
shredded lettuce

AMERICAN
4 hard-cooked eggs
¼ teaspoon dry mustard
2 teaspoons vinegar
1 tablespoon chutney
1 cup cottage cheese
¼ teaspoon salt
pinch of cayenne pepper or paprika
1 teaspoon chopped chives
To garnish:
parsley sprigs
shredded lettuce

Cut the eggs in half lengthways and remove the yolks. Mash with the mustard, vinegar and chutney. Add the cheese and mix well. Season to taste with salt and pepper or paprika and add the chives. Fill the egg whites with the mixture.

Arrange on a bed of shredded lettuce and garnish with parsley.

Serves 4

Stuffed Artichokes

METRIC/IMPERIAL	AMERICAN
4 large globe artichokes	*4 large globe artichokes*
25 g/1 oz butter	*2 tablespoons butter*
3 tablespoons oil	*3 tablespoons oil*
½ small onion, finely chopped	*½ small onion, finely chopped*
1 garlic clove, crushed	*1 garlic clove, crushed*
4 mushrooms, sliced	*4 mushrooms, sliced*
few small cauliflower florets	*few small cauliflower florets*

2 tablespoons wholewheat
  breadcrumbs
	2 tablespoons wholewheat
	  breadcrumbs

1 tablespoon chopped parsley	*1 tablespoon chopped parsley*
salt	*salt*
freshly ground black pepper	*freshly ground black pepper*
6 tablespoons dry white wine	*6 tablespoons dry white wine*

Cut off the stalks and trim the bases of the artichokes so that they stand upright. Pull off the coarse outer leaves and cut off the top third of the remaining leaves which are inedible. Pull the leaves back and remove the hairy 'choke' in the centre.

Heat the butter and 1 tablespoon of the oil in a small saucepan, add the onion, garlic, mushrooms and cauliflower and fry gently for 5 minutes, stirring frequently. Stir in the breadcrumbs, parsley, and salt and pepper to taste. Fill the artichokes with this mixture.

Heat the rest of the oil in a large pan. Stand the artichokes side by side in the pan. Add the wine, cover tightly and simmer over a very low heat for 40 minutes to 1 hour, until tender.
Serves 4

Eggs St Germain

METRIC/IMPERIAL	AMERICAN
500 g/1 lb frozen peas, cooked	*3 cups frozen peas, cooked*
25 g/1 oz butter	*2 tablespoons butter*
2 tablespoons double cream	*2 tablespoons heavy cream*
1 tablespoon chopped mint	*1 tablespoon chopped mint*
4 eggs	*4 eggs*

4 slices bread, toasted and cut into
  triangles
	4 slices bread, toasted and cut into
	  triangles

Place the peas, butter, cream and mint in an electric blender and work until smooth. Turn into a pan and heat gently.

Meanwhile, boil the eggs for 4 minutes and shell carefully.

Spoon the purée into 4 individual serving dishes. Place an egg in each and surround with toast triangles.
Serves 4

STUFFED ARTICHOKES

MAIN COURSES

EGG AND CHEESE DISHES
Potato Omelet

METRIC/IMPERIAL
*500 g/1 lb potatoes, cooked and
  mashed*
3 eggs, separated
100 g/4 oz Cheddar cheese, grated
2 tablespoons milk
1 tablespoon chopped parsley
salt
freshly ground black pepper
25 g/1 oz butter
To garnish:
cucumber slices
tomato slices
chopped parsley

AMERICAN
2 cups mashed potato
3 eggs, separated
1 cup grated Cheddar cheese
2 tablespoons milk
1 tablespoon chopped parsley
salt
freshly ground black pepper
2 tablespoons butter
To garnish:
cucumber slices
tomato slices
chopped parsley

Beat the potato with the egg yolks, cheese, milk, parsley, and salt and pepper to taste.

Whisk the egg whites until stiff and fold into the potato mixture.

Melt the butter in an omelet pan, add the mixture and cook for 2 minutes on each side.

Slide on to a serving plate and cut into quarters. Garnish each portion with cucumber and tomato and sprinkle with chopped parsley. Serve at once with a crisp green salad or vegetables.
Serves 4

30

Gnocchi with Tomato Sauce

METRIC/IMPERIAL
600 ml/1 pint milk
salt
freshly ground black pepper
175 g/6 oz semolina
100 g/4 oz Cheddar cheese, grated
1 egg, beaten
50 g/2 oz butter
Tomato sauce:
1 onion, chopped
1 carrot, chopped
15 g/½ oz wholewheat flour
300 ml/½ pint stock
500 g/1 lb tomatoes, skinned and
  chopped
1 bay leaf
1 garlic clove, peeled
1 teaspoon demerara sugar

AMERICAN
2½ cups milk
salt
freshly ground black pepper
1 cup semolina flour
1 cup grated Cheddar cheese
1 egg, beaten
¼ cup butter
Tomato sauce:
1 onion, chopped
1 carrot, chopped
1 tablespoon wholewheat flour
1¼ cups stock
2 cups skinned and chopped
  tomatoes
1 bay leaf
1 garlic clove, peeled
1 teaspoon raw sugar

Place the milk in a pan and bring to the boil. Season to taste with salt and pepper. Add the semolina and stir until the mixture thickens and leaves the sides of the pan.

Remove from the heat and stir in half of the cheese and the egg. Spread the mixture in a shallow dish to a depth of about 1 cm/½ inch and allow to cool. Cut into 2.5 cm/1 inch rounds or squares, arrange in a flameproof dish, sprinkle with the remaining cheese and dot with half of the butter. Keep on one side.

To prepare the sauce: melt the remaining butter in a saucepan. Add the onion and carrot and sauté for 5 minutes. Stir in the flour and cook for 1 minute. Add the remaining ingredients, with salt and pepper to taste, and bring to the boil, stirring. Lower the heat, cover and simmer for 30 minutes. Remove the bay leaf and garlic, cool slightly, then work in an electric blender or rub through a coarse sieve until smooth. Return to the pan and keep hot.

Brown the gnocchi under a preheated hot grill (broiler) for about 10 minutes, or until the top is golden. Serve with the tomato sauce.
Serves 4

Mushroom Scramble

METRIC/IMPERIAL	AMERICAN
225 g/8 oz button mushrooms	2 cups mushrooms
50 g/2 oz butter	¼ cup butter
4 tablespoons milk	¼ cup milk
10 eggs, lightly beaten	10 eggs, lightly beaten
sea salt	coarse salt
freshly ground black pepper	freshly ground black pepper

Leave 4 mushrooms whole and chop the rest. Melt 25 g/1 oz/2 tablespoons of the butter in a pan, add all the mushrooms and fry until softened.

Melt the remaining butter in another pan and add the milk. Season the eggs to taste with salt and pepper, pour into the pan and cook over a gentle heat, stirring constantly.

Add the chopped mushrooms when the eggs start to set and continue stirring. Transfer to a warmed shallow serving dish and garnish with the whole mushrooms.

Serve immediately, with crusty bread and a salad.
Serves 4

Cheese Pudding

METRIC/IMPERIAL	AMERICAN
300 ml/½ pint milk	1¼ cups milk
50 g/2 oz fresh wholewheat breadcrumbs	1 cup fresh wholewheat breadcrumbs
25 g/1 oz margarine	2 tablespoons margarine
salt	salt
freshly ground black pepper	freshly ground black pepper
350 g/12 oz cottage cheese, sieved	1½ cups cottage cheese, sieved
1 tablespoon grated onion	1 tablespoon grated onion
1 tablespoon chopped parsley	1 tablespoon chopped parsley
2 egg whites, stiffly whisked	2 egg whites, stiffly whisked

Warm the milk in a saucepan, remove from the heat and add the breadcrumbs, margarine, and salt and pepper to taste. Leave for 15 minutes to soften the breadcrumbs. Stir in the cheese, onion and parsley, then fold in the egg whites.

Spoon into a greased pie dish, place in a preheated moderately hot oven (200°C/400°F, Gas Mark 6) and cook for about 25 minutes, until well risen and golden; lower the heat slightly after 15 minutes if the pudding seems to be darkening too much. Serve immediately.
Serves 2 to 3

MUSHROOM SCRAMBLE; DEVILLED COTTAGE EGGS *(page 27)*;
MUSHROOM AND EGG RAMEKINS *(page 27)*

Oaty Cheese Quiche

METRIC/IMPERIAL
Pastry:
75 g/3 oz self-raising flour
125 g/5 oz fine oatmeal
100 g/4 oz butter
salt
freshly ground black pepper
water to mix
Filling:
350 g/12 oz cottage cheese, sieved
2 tablespoons natural yogurt
6 sticks celery, chopped
75 g/3 oz hazelnuts, chopped
pinch of curry powder
To garnish:
pinch of paprika
tomato slices
parsley sprigs

AMERICAN
Dough:
3/4 cup self-rising flour
1 cup fine oatmeal
1/2 cup butter
salt
freshly ground black pepper
water to mix
Filling:
1 × 3/4 lb carton ricotta cheese,
  sieved
2 tablespoons unflavored yogurt
6 celery stalks, chopped
3/4 cup chopped filberts
pinch of curry powder
To garnish:
pinch of paprika
tomato slices
parsley sprigs

Mix the flour and oatmeal together, with salt and freshly ground black pepper to taste. Cut in the butter and rub in until the mixture resembles breadcrumbs. Stir in enough water to make a fairly stiff pastry and knead together lightly.

Turn onto a floured surface, roll out and use to line a 23 cm/9 inch flan ring (pie pan). Cover the base with greaseproof (wax) paper and fill with dried beans. Place in a preheated moderately hot oven (200°C/400°F, Gas Mark 6) and bake 'blind' for 20 minutes. Remove the paper and beans and return to the oven for 5 minutes. Allow to cool.

Mix the cheese, yogurt, celery, nuts and curry powder together and pile into the flan case (pie shell). Sprinkle with paprika and garnish with tomato and parsley.
Serves 4 to 6

Corn and Asparagus Flan

METRIC/IMPERIAL
225 g/8 oz shortcrust pastry, made
 with 225 g/8 oz wholewheat flour
 (see method page 36)
1 × 198 g/7 oz can sweetcorn,
 drained
1 × 141 g/5 oz can asparagus tips,
 drained
1 small onion, chopped
75 g/3 oz Cheddar cheese, grated
2 large eggs, beaten
300 ml/½ pint milk
salt
freshly ground black pepper

AMERICAN
2 cups basic pie dough, made with
 2 cups wholewheat flour (see
 method page 36)
1 × 7 oz can kernel corn, drained
1 × 5 oz can asparagus tips,
 drained
1 small onion, chopped
¾ cup grated Cheddar cheese
2 large eggs, beaten
1¼ cups milk
salt
freshly ground black pepper

Roll out the prepared pastry (dough) and use to line a 20 cm/8 inch
flan tin (pie pan). Cover the base with greaseproof (wax) paper and
fill with dried beans. Place in a preheated moderately hot oven
(200°C/400°F, Gas Mark 6) and bake 'blind' for 10 minutes. Remove
the paper and beans and bake for a further 15 minutes.

Mix the corn, asparagus, onion, cheese, eggs and milk together.
Add salt and pepper to taste and pour into the prepared flan case (pie
shell). Lower the oven temperature to 190°C/375°F, Gas Mark 5 and
return to the oven for 30 minutes until set. Serve hot or cold.
Serves 4 to 6

Gouda Cheese Pie

METRIC/IMPERIAL
Shortcrust pastry:
225 g/8 oz plain flour
¼ teaspoon salt
25 g/1 oz lard
75 g/3 oz butter
water to mix
Filling:
25 g/1 oz butter
225 g/8 oz onions, finely sliced
12 stuffed green olives, sliced
2 eggs
300 ml/½ pint single cream
salt
freshly ground black pepper
100 g/4 oz Gouda cheese, grated

AMERICAN
Basic pie dough:
2 cups all-purpose flour
¼ teaspoon salt
2 tablespoons shortening
6 tablespoons butter
water to mix
Filling:
2 tablespoons butter
½ lb onions, finely sliced
12 stuffed green olives, sliced
2 eggs
1¼ cups light cream
salt
freshly ground black pepper
1 cup grated Gouda cheese

Sift the flour and salt into a bowl, cut in the lard (shortening) and butter and rub in until the mixture resembles breadcrumbs. Add just enough water to bind the mixture. Draw the pastry together to form a stiff dough and knead lightly until smooth.

Turn on to a floured surface, roll out and line a 23 cm/9 inch fluted flan tin (pie pan).

Melt the butter in a saucepan, add the onions and cook until soft but not browned. Lift the onions out with a slotted spoon, and place in the flan with the olives. Beat the eggs with the cream and seasoning and pour into the flan. Sprinkle with cheese and bake for 15 minutes in a preheated moderately hot oven (200°C/400°F, Gas Mark 6), then lower the heat to 180°C/350°F, Gas Mark 4, for a further 25 minutes or until golden brown and firm to the touch.
Serves 4

GOUDA CHEESE PIE
(Photograph: Olives from Spain)

Chakchouka

METRIC/IMPERIAL
2 tablespoons oil
2 onions, sliced
½ teaspoon chilli powder
2 red peppers, cored, seeded and
  sliced
2 green peppers, cored, seeded and
  sliced
6 tomatoes, skinned and chopped
salt
freshly ground black pepper
8 eggs

AMERICAN
2 tablespoons oil
2 onions, sliced
½ teaspoon chili powder
2 red peppers, cored, seeded and
  sliced
2 green peppers, cored, seeded and
  sliced
6 tomatoes, skinned and chopped
salt
freshly ground black pepper
8 eggs

Heat the oil in a frying pan (skillet), add the onions and fry until softened. Add the chilli powder and fry for 1 minute, then add the peppers, tomatoes and seasoning. Cover and simmer for 10 minutes.

Divide the mixture between 4 shallow ovenproof dishes and make 2 hollows in each. Break the eggs into the hollows and season to taste. Place in a preheated moderately hot oven (200°C/400°F, Gas Mark 6) and cook for 7 to 10 minutes, until the eggs are set.
Serves 4

Samsoe Flan

METRIC/IMPERIAL
175 g/6 oz shortcrust pastry, made
  with 175 g/6 oz wholewheat flour
  (see method page 36)
25 g/1 oz margarine
1 large onion, sliced
175 g/6 oz Samsoe cheese, grated
2 eggs, beaten
150 ml/¼ pint single cream
sea salt
freshly ground black pepper

AMERICAN
1½ cups basic pie dough, made
  with 1½ cups wholewheat flour
  (see method page 36)
2 tablespoons margarine
1 large onion, sliced
1½ cups grated Samsoe cheese
2 eggs, beaten
⅔ cup light cream
coarse salt
freshly ground black pepper

Roll out the prepared pastry (dough) and use to line an 18 cm/7 inch flan ring. Melt the margarine in a small pan, add the onion and fry until softened. Stir in the remaining ingredients, with salt and pepper to taste. Pour into the flan ring.

Place in a preheated moderately hot oven (200°C/400°F, Gas Mark 6) and bake for 20 minutes, then lower the heat to moderate (180°C/350°F, Gas Mark 4) and bake for 20 minutes until firm.
Serves 4 to 6

Pipérade

METRIC/IMPERIAL
3 tablespoons olive oil
2 onions, sliced
2 green peppers, cored, seeded and
  sliced
2 garlic cloves, crushed
3 large tomatoes, skinned, seeded
  and chopped
salt
freshly ground black pepper
8 eggs
3 tablespoons milk
15 g/½ oz margarine
To garnish:
garlic butter (see below)
3 small slices wholewheat bread,
  toasted

AMERICAN
3 tablespoons olive oil
2 onions, sliced
2 green peppers, cored, seeded and
  sliced
2 garlic cloves, crushed
3 large tomatoes, skinned, seeded
  and chopped
salt
freshly ground black pepper
8 eggs
3 tablespoons milk
1 tablespoon margarine
To garnish:
garlic butter (see below)
3 small slices wholewheat bread,
  toasted

Heat the oil in a large pan, add the onions and fry until softened. Add
the peppers and cook for 5 minutes, then add the garlic, tomatoes
and salt and pepper to taste. Simmer until all the ingredients are soft
and most of the liquid has evaporated.

Beat the eggs and milk together, with salt and pepper to taste.
Melt the margarine in a pan, add the eggs and scramble lightly.

Transfer the vegetables to a warmed serving dish, spread the eggs
on top and fork a little of the vegetable mixture into the edge of the
egg. Surround with small triangles of toast spread with garlic butter,
and serve immediately.

To prepare the garnish: soften 25 g/1 oz/2 tablespoons butter in a
bowl. Add crushed garlic to taste and beat well. Spread the toast
with the garlic butter and cut into 12 triangles.
Serves 6

Bean and Egg au Gratin

METRIC/IMPERIAL
500 g/1 lb shelled broad beans
salt
3 hard-boiled eggs, sliced
50 g/2 oz margarine
40 g/1½ oz wholewheat flour
450 ml/¾ pint milk
freshly ground black pepper
2 tablespoons fresh brown
  breadcrumbs
50 g/2 oz Cheddar cheese, grated

AMERICAN
1 lb shelled lima beans
salt
3 hard-cooked eggs, sliced
¼ cup margarine
6 tablespoons wholewheat flour
2 cups milk
freshly ground black pepper
2 tablespoons fresh brown
  breadcrumbs
½ cup grated Cheddar cheese

Cook the beans in boiling salted water until just tender; drain. Place half the beans in a greased ovenproof dish and place the eggs on top. Cover with the remaining beans.

Melt 40 g/1½ oz/3 tablespoons of the margarine in a pan, stir in the flour and cook gently, stirring, to make a roux. Remove from the heat and gradually add the milk, stirring. Return to the heat and bring to the boil. Cook, stirring, until thickened. Season to taste with salt and pepper.

Pour the sauce over the beans and sprinkle on the breadcrumbs and cheese. Dot with the remaining margarine, place in a preheated hot oven (220°C/425°F, Gas Mark 7) and cook for 15 minutes until golden brown. Serve immediately.
Serves 4

Wholewheat Pizza

METRIC/IMPERIAL
Dough:
25 g/1 oz fresh yeast
150 ml/¼ pint warm water
500 g/1 lb wholewheat flour
1 teaspoon salt
Topping:
6 tablespoons olive oil
3 onions, sliced
8 tomatoes, sliced
½ teaspoon oregano
salt
freshly ground black pepper
350 g/12 oz mozarella cheese,
 sliced
12 black olives, stoned

AMERICAN
Dough:
1 cake compressed yeast
⅔ cup warm water
4 cups wholewheat flour
1 teaspoon salt
Topping:
6 tablespoons olive oil
3 onions, sliced
8 tomatoes, sliced
½ teaspoon oregano
salt
freshly ground black pepper
¾ lb mozarella cheese, sliced
12 black olives, pitted

Cream the yeast with a little of the water and stir until dissolved. Put the flour in a bowl with the salt, add the yeast mixture with the remaining water and mix to a firm dough.

Turn onto a floured surface and knead for 8 minutes until smooth and elastic. Return to the bowl, cover with a damp cloth and leave to rise in a warm place until it has doubled in bulk.

Turn onto a floured surface, knead for 2 minutes, then shape into two 23 cm/9 inch rounds and place on a greased baking sheet.

Heat 4 tablespoons of the oil in a pan and fry the onions until softened. Cool slightly, then spoon the onions on to the two rounds of dough. Arrange the tomatoes over the onions, and sprinkle with oregano, salt and pepper. Lay the cheese on top and scatter over the olives. Pour the remaining oil over each pizza and bake them in a preheated moderately hot oven (200°C/400°F, Gas Mark 6) for 20 minutes.

Makes two 23 cm/9 inch pizzas

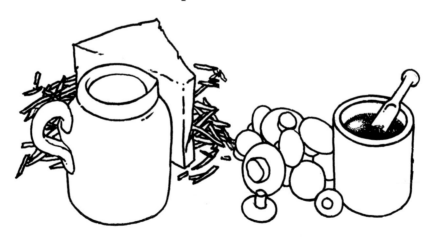

Wholewheat Tomato Quiche

METRIC/IMPERIAL

Shortcrust pastry:
225 g/8 oz wholewheat flour
½ teaspoon salt
50 g/2 oz lard
50 g/2 oz margarine
water to mix
Filling:
2 hard-boiled eggs, chopped
75 g/3 oz Cheshire cheese, grated
1 tablespoon snipped chives
8 small tomatoes, skinned and cut
 in half
2 large eggs
200 ml/⅓ pint milk
4 tablespoons single cream
salt
freshly ground black pepper
parsley sprigs to garnish

AMERICAN

Basic pie dough:
2 cups wholewheat flour
½ teaspoon salt
¼ cup shortening
¼ cup margarine
water to mix
Filling:
2 hard-cooked eggs, chopped
¾ cup grated Cheddar cheese
1 tablespoon snipped chives
8 small tomatoes, skinned and cut
 in half
2 large eggs
⅞ cup milk
¼ cup light cream
salt
freshly ground black pepper
parsley sprigs to garnish

Sift the flour and salt into a bowl, cut in the lard (shortening) and margarine and rub in until the mixture resembles breadcrumbs. Add just enough water to bind the mixture. Draw the pastry together to form a stiff dough and knead lightly until smooth.

Turn onto a floured surface, roll out to a 25 cm/10 inch circle and use to line a 20 cm/8 inch flan ring (pie pan) standing on a baking (cookie) sheet.

Cover the base with the chopped hard-boiled egg, then sprinkle with the cheese and chives. Arrange the tomatoes on top.

Beat the eggs with the milk, cream and salt and pepper to taste and pour over the tomatoes.

Place in a preheated hot oven (220°C/425°F, Gas Mark 7) and cook for 15 minutes, then lower the heat to 180°C/350°F, Gas Mark 4 and cook for a further 25 minutes or until golden brown and firm to the touch. Garnish with parsley and serve hot or cold with salad.
Serves 4 to 6

West Country Gratin

METRIC/IMPERIAL
50 g/2 oz butter
500 g/1 lb onions, sliced
salt
freshly ground black pepper
25 g/1 oz wholewheat flour
300 ml/½ pint milk
1 teaspoon made English mustard
100 g/4 oz Cheddar cheese, grated
6 large eggs, hard-boiled and sliced
2 slices bread, toasted
tomato slices to garnish

AMERICAN
¼ cup butter
1 lb onions, sliced
salt
freshly ground black pepper
¼ cup wholewheat flour
1¼ cups milk
1 teaspoon prepared English
  mustard
1 cup grated Cheddar cheese
6 large eggs, hard-cooked and sliced
2 slices bread, toasted
tomato slices to garnish

Melt half of the butter in a saucepan, add the onions and cook for 5 minutes, stirring, until soft. Season to taste with salt and pepper. Turn into a 900 ml/1½ pint/3¾ cup ovenproof dish and keep warm.

Melt the remaining butter in a pan, add the flour and mix well. Remove from the heat, pour on the milk and mix thoroughly. Return to the heat and cook, stirring, until the sauce thickens and comes to the boil. Stir in the mustard and season to taste with salt and freshly ground black pepper. Add three-quarters of the cheese and stir well.

Arrange the eggs on top of the onions, pour over the sauce and sprinkle with the remaining cheese. Place under a preheated hot grill (broiler) until golden and bubbling.

Cut the toast into triangles and arrange around the edge of the dish. Garnish with tomato and serve at once.
Serves 4

PEAR AND GRAPE SALAD *(page 24)*

Tomato Eggs with Brown Rice

METRIC/IMPERIAL	AMERICAN
50 g/2 oz butter	*¼ cup butter*
225 g/8 oz brown rice, cooked	*1 cup brown rice, cooked*
4 hard-boiled eggs, halved	*4 hard-cooked eggs, halved*
Tomato Sauce:	**Tomato Sauce:**
1 onion, chopped	*1 onion, chopped*
1 garlic clove, crushed	*1 garlic clove, minced*
1 × 396 g/14 oz can tomatoes	*1 × 14 oz can tomatoes*
pinch each of sugar, salt, basil and freshly ground black pepper	*pinch each of sugar, salt, basil and freshly ground black pepper*
2 tablespoons double cream	*2 tablespoons heavy cream*

Grease a 20 cm/8 inch ring mould with some of the butter and fill with the cooked rice, packing down firmly. Leave to set while preparing the tomato sauce.

Melt the remaining butter in a pan, add the onion and fry until softened. Add the garlic, tomatoes with their juice and seasonings. Cover and simmer for 5 to 10 minutes. Cool slightly, then work in an electric blender or rub through a coarse sieve to make a purée.

Return to the pan and stir in the cream. Add the eggs and heat gently. Turn the rice ring onto a serving dish and spoon the tomato mixture into the centre.

Serves 4

Baked Stuffed Courgettes (Zucchini)

METRIC/IMPERIAL	AMERICAN
4 large courgettes	*4 large zucchini*
2 large eggs, beaten	*2 large eggs, beaten*
1 × 326 g/11½ oz can sweetcorn drained	*1 × 11½ oz can kernel corn drained*
1 large onion, chopped	*1 large onion, chopped*
100 g/4 oz black olives, stoned and quartered	*¾ cup pitted black olives, quartered*
75 g/3 oz Cheddar cheese, grated	*¾ cup grated Cheddar cheese*
salt	*salt*
freshly ground black pepper	*freshly ground black pepper*

Blanch the courgettes (zucchini) in boiling water to cover for 3 minutes. Drain and cool slightly. Cut in half lengthways, scoop out and chop the flesh. Mix with the remaining ingredients, adding salt and pepper to taste, and pile back into the courgette (zucchini) shells. Place in a shallow baking dish and cook in a preheated moderate oven (180°C/350°F, Gas Mark 4) for 35 minutes. Serve hot.

Serves 4

NUT AND PULSE DISHES

Tomato and Walnut Casserole

METRIC/IMPERIAL
75 g/3 oz wholewheat macaroni
salt
350 g/12 oz tomatoes, skinned and
  chopped
freshly ground black pepper
2 teaspoons grated onion
2 bay leaves
100 g/4 oz Cheddar cheese, grated
100 g/4 oz walnut halves, chopped

AMERICAN
3/4 cup wholewheat macaroni
salt
1 1/2 cups skinned and chopped
  tomatoes
freshly ground black pepper
2 teaspoons grated onion
2 bay leaves
1 cup grated Cheddar cheese
1 cup chopped walnuts

Cook the macaroni in boiling, salted water until just tender. Drain thoroughly.

Put the tomatoes in a saucepan with a little salt, pepper to taste, the onion and bay leaves. Cook slowly, stirring frequently, until a thick purée is formed. Remove the bay leaves.

Butter an ovenproof dish and fill with alternate layers of macaroni, tomato purée, cheese and walnuts, finishing with tomato and cheese.

Place in a moderately hot oven (200°C/400°F, Gas Mark 6) and cook for approximately 25 minutes, until the cheese topping is golden.

Serve with a green salad.

Serves 4

Peanut Roast

METRIC/IMPERIAL
225 g/8 oz whole shelled peanuts
50 g/2 oz vegetarian fat
2 onions, chopped
1 large tomato, skinned and
  chopped
2 small dessert apples, peeled and
  diced
25 g/1 oz oatmeal
1 teaspoon chopped sage
sea salt
freshly ground black pepper
1 egg
little milk
To garnish:
tomato slices
cucumber slices
parsley sprigs

AMERICAN
1⅛ cups whole shelled peanuts
¼ cup shortening
2 onions, chopped
1 large tomato, skinned and
  chopped
2 small dessert apples, peeled and
  diced
2⅔ tablespoons oatmeal
1 teaspoon chopped sage
coarse salt
freshly ground black pepper
1 egg
little milk
To garnish:
tomato slices
cucumber slices
parsley sprigs

Chop, mince or grind the peanuts. Heat the fat in a pan, add the onions, tomato and apples and fry until softened. Add the peanuts, oatmeal, sage, and salt and pepper to taste. Bind with the egg and just enough milk to give a fairly moist consistency.

Press into a greased 500 g/1 lb/8 × 4½ × 2½ inch loaf tin (pan) and cover with greased foil. Place in a preheated moderate oven (180°C/350°F, Gas Mark 4) and cook for 45 minutes to 1 hour.

Transfer to a warmed serving dish and garnish with tomato, cucumber and parsley. Serve with a green vegetable or salad.
Serves 4

Rice and Peanut Roast
Use recipe above, but cook 50 g/2 oz/⅓ cup brown or white rice and blend with peanuts, etc., before adding the milk. Cook as above; do not turn out of dish.

Savoury Peanut Pie

METRIC/IMPERIAL
2 tablespoons groundnut oil
1 large onion, sliced
225 g/8 oz roasted peanuts,
  chopped
1 × 226 g/8 oz can tomatoes
1 teaspoon Worcestershire sauce
1 teaspoon chopped mixed herbs
salt
freshly ground black pepper
225 g/8 oz shortcrust pastry, made
  with 225 g/8 oz wholewheat flour
  (see method page 36)
1 egg, beaten

AMERICAN
2 tablespoons groundnut oil
1 large onion, sliced
2 cups chopped roasted peanuts
1 × ½ lb can tomatoes
1 teaspoon Worcestershire sauce
1 teaspoon chopped mixed herbs
salt
freshly ground black pepper
2 cups basic pie dough, made with
  2 cups wholewheat flour (see
  method page 36)
1 egg, beaten

Heat the oil in a frying pan (skillet), add the onion and fry for about 10 minutes until softened. Stir in the nuts, tomatoes with their juice, Worcestershire sauce, herbs, and salt and pepper to taste. Bring to the boil and simmer for 2 to 3 minutes. Remove from the heat and leave to cool.

Divide the prepared pastry (dough) in half. Roll out one piece on a floured surface and use to line a 20 cm/8 inch pie plate. Spoon in the filling. Roll out the remaining pastry (dough) and use to cover the pie. Knock up the edges, seal well and flute. Use any pastry trimmings to decorate the pie. Brush with beaten egg.

Place in a preheated moderately hot oven (200°C/400°F, Gas Mark 6) and bake for 35 to 40 minutes, until golden. Serve hot or cold, with vegetables of your choice or salad.

Serves 4

Bean and Tomato Hot-Pot

METRIC/IMPERIAL
2 tablespoons oil
2 onions, sliced
3 carrots, sliced
2 sticks celery, sliced
1 large leek, sliced
2 garlic cloves, crushed
1 × 425 g/15 oz can red kidney
  beans, drained
1 × 396 g/14 oz can tomatoes
300 ml/½ pint stock
1 tablespoon yeast extract
sea salt
freshly ground black pepper
750 g/1½ lb potatoes, thinly sliced
15 g/½ oz butter

AMERICAN
2 tablespoons oil
2 onions, sliced
3 carrots, sliced
2 celery stalks, sliced
1 large leek, sliced
2 garlic cloves, crushed
1 × 15 oz can red kidney beans,
  drained
1 × 14 oz can tomatoes
1¼ cups stock
1 tablespoon brewer's yeast
coarse salt
freshly ground black pepper
1½ lb potatoes, thinly sliced
1 tablespoon butter

Heat the oil in a flameproof casserole, add the onions and fry for 5 minutes. Add the carrots, celery, leek and garlic and fry for a further 5 minutes.

Add the kidney beans, tomatoes with their juice, stock, yeast extract (brewer's yeast), and salt and pepper to taste. Mix well.

Arrange the potatoes neatly on top, sprinkling salt and pepper between each layer. Dot with the butter, cover, place in a preheated moderate oven (180°C/350°F, Gas Mark 4) and cook for 2 hours. Remove the lid 30 minutes before the end of cooking to allow the potatoes to brown.
Serves 4

Nut and Vegetable Loaf

METRIC/IMPERIAL
25 g/1 oz butter
1 small onion, chopped
1 small carrot, chopped
1 stick celery, chopped
1 tablespoon tomato purée
225 g/8 oz tomatoes, skinned and
  chopped
2 eggs
1 tablespoon chopped parsley
salt
freshly ground black pepper
225 g/8 oz nuts, finely chopped or
  minced
To garnish:
onion rings
parsley sprigs

AMERICAN
2 tablespoons butter
1 small onion, chopped
1 small carrot, chopped
1 celery stalk, chopped
1 tablespoon tomato paste
1 cup skinned and chopped tomatoes
2 eggs
1 tablespoon chopped parsley
salt
freshly ground black pepper
2 cups finely chopped or ground
  nuts
To garnish:
onion rings
parsley sprigs

Melt the butter in a pan, add the onion, carrot and celery and cook until softened. Add the tomato purée (paste) and tomatoes and cook for 5 minutes.

Put the eggs, parsley and salt and pepper to taste in a bowl and beat well. Stir in the nuts and vegetables.

Transfer to a greased 900 ml/1½ pint/3¾ cup ovenproof dish, place in preheated hot oven (220°C/425°F, Gas Mark 7) and bake for 30 to 35 minutes.

Turn out and decorate with onion rings and parsley. Serve hot with vegetables and sauce, or cold with salad.
Serves 4 to 6

MUSHROOM AND SPINACH SALAD *(page 78)*;
HOT POTATO SALAD *(page 78)*

Fruit and Nut Risotto

METRIC/IMPERIAL	AMERICAN
4 tablespoons oil	¼ cup oil
225 g/8 oz brown rice	1 generous cup brown rice
2 onions, chopped	2 onions, chopped
1 green pepper, cored, seeded and chopped	1 green pepper, cored, seeded and chopped
100 g/4 oz cashew nuts	1 cup cashew nuts
225 g/8 oz mushrooms, sliced	2 cups sliced mushrooms
4 tomatoes, skinned and chopped	4 tomatoes, skinned and chopped
50 g/2 oz raisins	⅓ cup raisins
salt	salt
freshly ground black pepper	freshly ground black pepper

Heat half of the oil in a large pan. Add the rice and fry for 3 minutes. Cover with boiling water and cook for 45 minutes; drain well.

Heat the remaining oil in a frying pan (skillet), add the onions and fry until softened. Add the pepper, nuts and mushrooms and cook for 6 to 7 minutes. Add the cooked rice, tomatoes, raisins, and salt and pepper to taste and reheat gently.

Serves 4

Lentils au Gratin

METRIC/IMPERIAL	AMERICAN
2 tablespoons oil	2 tablespoons oil
2 onions, chopped	2 onions, chopped
2 carrots, chopped	2 carrots, chopped
2 sticks celery, chopped	2 celery stalks, chopped
600 ml/1 pint stock	2½ cups stock
225 g/8 oz red lentils	1 cup red lentils
1 tablespoon yeast extract	1 tablespoon brewer's yeast
salt	salt
freshly ground black pepper	freshly ground black pepper
1 tablespoon chopped parsley	1 tablespoon chopped parsley
Topping:	**Topping:**
100 g/4 oz Cheddar cheese, grated	1 cup grated Cheddar cheese
2 tablespoons wholewheat breadcrumbs	2 tablespoons wholewheat breadcrumbs

Heat the oil in a pan, add the onion, carrot and celery and fry for 5 minutes. Add the remaining ingredients and simmer gently for 45 to 50 minutes, stirring occasionally.

Turn into a buttered pie dish and sprinkle the cheese and bread-crumbs on top. Place under a preheated hot grill (broiler) for about 5 minutes, until golden. Serve immediately.

Serves 4

VEGETABLE DISHES

Potato Timbale

METRIC/IMPERIAL
1 kg/2 lb potatoes, cooked and
  mashed
2 egg yolks
pinch of grated nutmeg
25 g/1 oz butter
500 g/1 lb cooked mixed vegetables,
  e.g. mushrooms, peas, beans,
  cauliflower, broccoli, Brussels
  sprouts
4 hard-boiled eggs, sliced
parsley sprigs to garnish
Cheese sauce:
50 g/2 oz Cheddar cheese, grated
pinch of mustard
1-2 drops Worcestershire sauce
150 ml/¼ pint white sauce

AMERICAN
4 cups mashed potato
2 egg yolks
pinch of grated nutmeg
2 tablespoons butter
1 lb cooked mixed vegetables, e.g.
  mushrooms, peas, beans,
  cauliflower, broccoli, Brussels
  sprouts
4 hard-cooked eggs, sliced
parsley sprigs to garnish
Cheese sauce:
½ cup grated Cheddar cheese
pinch of mustard
1-2 drops Worcestershire sauce
⅔ cup white sauce

Beat the potato, egg yolks, nutmeg and butter together. Place three-quarters of the mixture in a piping (pastry) bag fitted with a large nozzle and pipe around the edge of a 1.2 litre/2 pint/5 cup pie dish.

To make the cheese sauce, add the cheese, mustard and Worcestershire sauce to the hot white sauce and stir gently, off the heat, until the cheese has melted.

Put the vegetables and hard-boiled eggs in a pan, pour over the sauce and heat gently. Pour into the pie dish.

Pipe the remaining potato over the filling in a decorative pattern. Place under a preheated grill (broiler) for 4 minutes until golden. Serve immediately, garnished with parsley.
Serves 6

Vegetable Curry

METRIC/IMPERIAL
4 tablespoons oil
2 onions, sliced
1 garlic clove, crushed
1 tablespoon curry powder
1 teaspoon turmeric
1 small cauliflower, broken into
 florets
4 carrots, sliced
2 medium turnips, diced
1 tablespoon tomato purée
300 ml/½ pint stock
salt
1 × 141 g/5 oz carton natural
 yogurt
1 tablespoon chopped parsley

AMERICAN
¼ cup oil
2 onions, sliced
1 garlic clove, crushed
1 tablespoon curry powder
1 teaspoon turmeric
1 small cauliflower, broken into
 florets
4 carrots, sliced
2 medium turnips, diced
1 tablespoon tomato paste
1¼ cups stock
salt
⅔ cup unflavored yogurt
1 tablespoon chopped parsley

Heat the oil in a pan, add the onions and fry for 5 minutes until softened. Add the garlic, curry powder and turmeric and cook for a further 2 minutes.

Add the cauliflower, carrot, turnip, tomato purée (paste), stock, and salt to taste. Cover and simmer gently for 40 to 45 minutes until the vegetables are tender. Stir in the yogurt and reheat gently; do not boil. Sprinkle with parsley to serve.
Serves 4

Vegetable Crumble

METRIC/IMPERIAL	AMERICAN
190 g/6½ oz wholewheat flour	*1½ cups plus 2 tablespoons*
100 g/4 oz butter	*wholewheat flour*
75 g/3 oz Danish blue cheese,	*½ cup butter*
grated	*¾ cup grated Danish blue cheese*
225 g/8 oz onions, sliced	*½ lb onions, sliced*
175 g/6 oz carrots, sliced	*1¼ cups sliced carrots*
4 sticks celery, chopped	*4 celery stalks, chopped*
3 teaspoons yeast extract	*3 teaspoons brewer's yeast*
450 ml/¾ pint boiling water	*2 cups boiling water*
500 g/1 lb cabbage, shredded	*6 cups finely chopped cabbage*
225 g/8 oz tomatoes, skinned and	*½ lb tomatoes, skinned and sliced*
sliced	*salt*
salt	*freshly ground black pepper*
freshly ground black pepper	

Sift 150 g/5 oz/1¼ cups of the flour into a mixing bowl. Rub in half the butter, then stir in the cheese. Set aside.

Melt the remaining butter in a large frying pan (skillet), and cook the onions, carrots and celery for 10 minutes until soft but not brown. Stir in the remaining flour and cook for 2 minutes.

Dissolve the yeast extract (brewer's yeast) in the boiling water and add to the pan. Cook, stirring until thickened, then add the remaining vegetables and salt and pepper to taste.

Pour into a casserole and sprinkle the crumble over the top. Place in a preheated moderate oven (180°C/350°F, Gas Mark 4) and cook for 1 hour until the topping is golden.

Serves 6

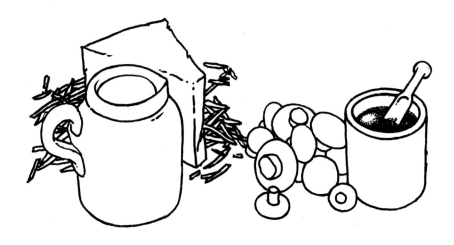

Marrow (Squash) Casserole

METRIC/IMPERIAL	AMERICAN
2 tablespoons oil	2 tablespoons oil
2 onions, sliced	2 onions, sliced
1 green pepper, cored, seeded and sliced	1 green pepper, cored, seeded and sliced
275 g/9 oz brown rice	1¼ cups brown rice
1 kg/2 lb marrow, peeled, seeds removed and cut into cubes	2 lb squash, peeled, seeds removed and cut into cubes
1 × 396 g/14 oz can tomatoes	1 × 14 oz can tomatoes
2 tablespoons tomato purée	2 tablespoons tomato paste
300 ml/½ pint stock	1¼ cups stock
2 teaspoons yeast extract	2 teaspoons brewer's yeast
salt	salt
freshly ground black pepper	freshly ground black pepper

Heat the oil in a flameproof casserole, add the onion and fry for 5 minutes. Add the pepper and rice and cook for a further 2 to 3 minutes, stirring. Add the marrow (squash), tomatoes, tomato purée (paste), stock, yeast extract (brewer's yeast) and salt and pepper to taste. Mix well.

Cover, place in a preheated moderate oven (180°C/350°F, Gas Mark 4) and cook for 1 to 1¼ hours.
Serves 4

Green Pancakes (Crêpes)

METRIC/IMPERIAL	AMERICAN
100 g/4 oz sorrel or spinach	¼ lb sorrel or spinach
100 g/4 oz wholewheat flour	1 cup wholewheat flour
sea salt	coarse salt
1 egg	1 egg
150 ml/¼ pint milk	⅔ cup milk
oil for frying	oil for frying
Filling:	**Filling:**
500 g/1 lb cream cheese	2 cups cream cheese
4 tablespoons snipped chives	¼ cup snipped chives

Cook the sorrel (or spinach) leaves in a saucepan with a little water, then push through a coarse sieve to make a thin purée.

Sift the flour and a pinch of salt into a bowl. Beat in the egg and milk, then the purée. Allow the batter to stand for a little before using. Mix the cream cheese with the chives.

Heat a little oil in a frying pan (skillet) and use the batter to make 8 to 10 small pancakes (crêpes). Put about 2 tablespoons of the cheese filling in each pancake (crêpe) and roll them up. Serve immediately.
Serves 4

Herb Gnocchi

METRIC/IMPERIAL	AMERICAN
225 g/8 oz spinach	*½ lb spinach*
100 g/4 oz sorrel	*¼ lb sorrel*
1 bunch watercress	*1 bunch American cress*
50 g/2 oz parsley	*1½ cups parsley*
1 tablespoon chopped chervil	*1 tablespoon chopped chervil*
1 tablespoon chopped tarragon	*1 tablespoon chopped tarragon*
1 tablespoon chopped dill	*1 tablespoon chopped dill*
175 g/6 oz ricotta cheese	*⅔ cup ricotta cheese*
25 g/1 oz butter, diced	*2 tablespoons butter, diced*
75 g/3 oz Parmesan cheese, grated	*¾ cup freshly grated Parmesan*
sea salt	*cheese*
freshly ground black pepper	*coarse salt*
2 eggs, beaten	*freshly ground black pepper*
3 tablespoons plain flour, sifted	*2 eggs, beaten*
melted butter to serve (optional)	*3 tablespoons all-purpose flour, sifted*
	melted butter to serve (optional)

Wash and drain the spinach, sorrel, watercress (American cress) and parsley. Place in a large pan of boiling water and boil for 4 minutes; drain. When cool enough to handle, press out as much moisture as possible and chop finely. Add the remaining herbs and place in a saucepan over a low heat for several minutes, stirring, to dry out.

Beat the ricotta cheese to a smooth consistency and add to the purée with the butter, 25 g/1 oz/¼ cup of the Parmesan cheese and salt and pepper to taste. Take the pan off the heat and stir in the eggs and flour. Beat until smooth. Pour into a cool shallow dish and leave in the refrigerator overnight.

Bring a large pan of lightly salted water to the boil. Form the green mixture into egg-shaped gnocchi, using 2 teaspoons, and roll them very lightly on a floured board. Drop them in batches in the pan, but do not crowd them.

When they float to the surface, after 4 to 5 minutes, lift them out with a slotted spoon and drain on a cloth. Test one to make sure they are cooked through, then transfer to a warmed serving dish while you cook the others.

Sprinkle the gnocchi with a little Parmesan cheese; serve the remaining cheese separately. Serve with melted butter if liked.
Serves 4

HERB GNOCCHI; GREEN PANCAKES (CRÊPES) *(page 59)*

Spinach Quiche

METRIC/IMPERIAL

225 g/8 oz shortcrust pastry, made
* with 225 g/8 oz wholewheat flour*
* (see method page 36)*
1 egg yolk, beaten
Filling:
225 g/8 oz spinach
50 g/2 oz parsley
2 eggs
300 ml/½ pint single cream
salt
freshly ground black pepper
50 g/2 oz Parmesan cheese, grated

AMERICAN

2 cups basic pie dough, made with
* 2 cups wholewheat flour*
* (see method page 36)*
1 egg yolk, beaten
Filling:
½ lb spinach
1½ cups parsley
2 eggs
1¼ cups light cream
salt
freshly ground black pepper
½ cup freshly grated Parmesan
* cheese*

Roll out the prepared pastry (dough) and use to line a 23 cm/9 inch
flan tin (pie pan). Cover the base with greaseproof (wax) paper and fill
with dried beans. Place in a moderately hot oven (200°C/400°F, Gas
Mark 6) and bake 'blind' for 10 minutes. Remove the paper and
beans, brush the pastry all over with egg yolk and return to the oven
for 5 minutes. Leave to cool.

Put the spinach and parsley in a large pan of boiling water and boil
for 4 minutes. Drain well, pressing out the moisture with the back of
a wooden spoon. Cool and finely chop.

Beat the eggs in a bowl, add the cream and mix well. Add salt and
pepper to taste, the spinach mixture and most of the cheese,
reserving a little to sprinkle over the top.

Pour into the flan case (pie shell) and sprinkle the reserved cheese
over the top. Place in a moderate oven (180°C/350°F, Gas Mark 4)
and bake for 30 minutes. Serve immediately.
Serves 4

Mushroom Flans

METRIC/IMPERIAL
*225 g/8 oz shortcrust pastry, made
  with 225 g/8 oz wholewheat flour
  (see method page 36)*
Filling:
*50 g/2 oz butter
500 g/1 lb flat mushrooms
1 tablespoon plain flour
200 ml/⅓ pint stock
6 tablespoons soured cream
salt
freshly ground black pepper
lemon juice
½ tablespoon chopped parsley
½ tablespoon snipped chives*

AMERICAN
*2 cups basic pie dough, made with
  2 cups wholewheat flour
  (see method page 36)*
Filling:
*¼ cup butter
1 lb flat mushrooms
1 tablespoon all-purpose flour
⅞ cup stock
6 tablespoons sour cream
salt
freshly ground black pepper
lemon juice
½ tablespoon chopped parsley
½ tablespoon snipped chives*

Roll out the pastry (dough) thinly and use to line four 7.5-10 cm/
3-4 inch patty tins (muffin pans). Lay a small piece of greased foil in
each one, and fill with a few dried beans. Place in a moderately hot
oven (200°C/400°F, Gas Mark 6) and bake 'blind' for 10 minutes.
Remove the foil and beans and return to the oven for a further 5 to
10 minutes.

Meanwhile, melt 40 g/1½ oz/3 tablespoons of the butter in a pan,
add the mushrooms and cook gently, stirring once or twice, until
softened. Drain off the juice and remove the pan from the heat.

Melt the remaining butter in a clean pan and stir in the flour. Add
the stock and sour cream and cook for 3 minutes, stirring constantly.
Add salt, pepper and lemon juice to taste, then mix in the
mushrooms. Reheat the mixture, stir in the herbs and divide between
the pastry shells. Serve immediately.
Serves 4

VEGETABLES

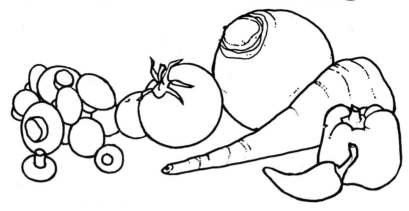

Chinese Cabbage (Bok Choy) with Onion and Tomato

METRIC/IMPERIAL	AMERICAN
1 medium head Chinese cabbage, quartered	1 medium head bok choy, quartered
sea salt	coarse salt
50 g/2 oz butter	1/4 cup butter
150 ml/1/4 pint stock	2/3 cup stock
freshly ground black pepper	freshly ground black pepper
1 onion, sliced	1 onion, sliced
1 garlic clove, crushed	1 garlic clove, crushed
100 g/4 oz tomatoes, skinned, seeded and chopped	1/2 cup skinned, seeded and chopped tomatoes
1 tablespoon chopped parsley	1 tablespoon chopped parsley

Put the cabbage (bok choy) in a pan of boiling salted water and cook for 5 minutes; drain well.

Melt half the butter in a pan just big enough to take the cabbage (bok choy) quarters in one layer. Add the cabbage (bok choy), stock and salt and pepper to taste. Cover and cook slowly for 10 minutes.

Meanwhile, melt the remaining butter in a pan, add the onion and cook until softened. Add the garlic, tomatoes, parsley and salt and pepper to taste. Cook for a further 5 minutes.

Strain the cabbage (bok choy) and add a little of the liquid to the tomato mixture. Boil rapidly until thickened.

Place the Chinese cabbage (bok choy) in a warmed serving dish and pour the tomato sauce on top.

Serves 4

CHINESE CABBAGE (BOK CHOY) WITH ONION AND TOMATO; RED CABBAGE ALLEMANDE (page 67)

Asparagus with Peas

METRIC/IMPERIAL
500 g/1 lb fresh asparagus tips
salt
500 g/1 lb shelled peas
Sauce:
50 g/2 oz butter
2 tablespoons wholewheat flour
300 ml/½ pint milk
1 tablespoon chopped mint
1 tablespoon chopped parsley
freshly ground white pepper
To serve:
few triangles of bread, fried in
  butter

AMERICAN
1 lb fresh asparagus tips
salt
3 cups shelled peas
Sauce:
¼ cup butter
2 tablespoons wholewheat flour
1¼ cups milk
1 tablespoon chopped mint
1 tablespoon chopped parsley
freshly ground white pepper
To serve:
few triangles of bread, fried in
  butter

Cook the asparagus tips in boiling salted water for 2 to 3 minutes. Drain thoroughly and mix with the peas.

To make the sauce: melt the butter in a saucepan over low heat. Stir in the flour and cook, stirring, for 1 to 2 minutes. Gradually add the milk and cook, stirring, until thickened. Add the herbs, and salt and pepper to taste.

Stir in the asparagus and peas and cook gently for 15 minutes or until tender, stirring frequently. Add a little milk if the sauce becomes too thick.

Transfer to a warmed serving dish and garnish with bread triangles to serve.
Serves 4

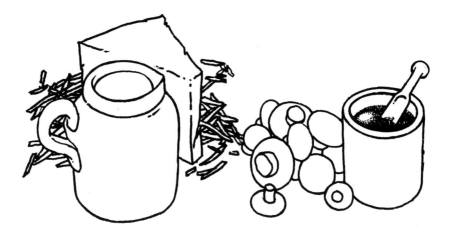

Red Cabbage Allemande

METRIC/IMPERIAL
500 g/1 lb red cabbage, shredded
25 g/1 oz butter
1 large onion, sliced
1 medium cooking apple, peeled,
  cored and sliced
1 tablespoon Muscovado sugar
1 teaspoon sea salt
2 tablespoons red wine vinegar
freshly ground black pepper

AMERICAN
6 cups shredded red cabbage
2 tablespoons butter
1 large onion, sliced
1 medium cooking apple, peeled,
  cored and sliced
1 tablespoon Barbados sugar
1 teaspoon coarse salt
2 tablespoons red wine vinegar
freshly ground black pepper

Blanch the cabbage in boiling water to cover for 4 minutes. Drain well, reserving the liquid.

Melt the butter in a pan, add the onion and apple and cook for 3 minutes. Add the cabbage, sugar, salt, vinegar, pepper to taste, and 4 tablespoons (¼ cup) of the reserved cabbage water.

Bring to the boil, cover and simmer for 15 minutes, stirring occasionally.

Transfer to a warmed serving dish and serve immediately.
Serves 4

Spiced Cauliflower

METRIC/IMPERIAL
1 teaspoon each of cumin, coriander
  and mustard seeds
1 tablespoon olive oil
1 teaspoon salt
½ teaspoon turmeric
pinch of cayenne pepper
1 large cauliflower, broken into
  florets
3 onions, chopped
4 carrots, sliced
120 ml/4 fl oz water
300 ml/½ pint natural yogurt

AMERICAN
1 teaspoon each of cumin, coriander
  and mustard seeds
1 tablespoon olive oil
1 teaspoon salt
½ teaspoon turmeric
pinch of cayenne pepper
1 large cauliflower, broken into
  florets
3 onions, chopped
4 carrots, sliced
½ cup water
1¼ cups unflavored yogurt

Grind or crush the whole spices. Heat the oil in a pan, add the ground spices and cook gently for 4 minutes. Add the salt, turmeric, cayenne and vegetables and cook gently, stirring, for 5 minutes. Stir in the water, cover and simmer until the vegetables are tender. Stir in the yogurt and reheat gently. Serve with crusty bread.
Serves 4

Stir-fried Bean Shoots

METRIC/IMPERIAL	AMERICAN
3 tablespoons oil	*3 tablespoons oil*
2-3 garlic cloves, crushed	*2-3 garlic cloves, crushed*
2 slices root ginger, shredded	*2 slices ginger root, shredded*
500 g/1 lb fresh bean sprouts	*1 lb fresh bean sprouts*
sea salt	*coarse salt*
freshly ground black pepper	*freshly ground black pepper*
1½ tablespoons soy sauce	*1½ tablespoons soy sauce*
3 spring onions, cut into 5 cm/	*3 scallions, cut into 2 inch pieces*
* 2 inch pieces*	*1½ teaspoons sesame oil*
1½ teaspoons sesame seed oil	

Heat the oil in a pan. Add the garlic and ginger and stir-fry for a few seconds. Add the bean sprouts and sprinkle with salt and pepper to taste. Turn the bean sprouts quickly so that they become evenly coated with oil. Add the soy sauce and spring onions (scallions).

Continue to stir-fry over high heat for 2 minutes. Sprinkle with the sesame oil and serve immediately.
Serves 4

Corn Fritters

METRIC/IMPERIAL	AMERICAN
3 large eggs, separated	*3 large eggs, separated*
50 g/2 oz wholewheat flour	*½ cup wholewheat flour*
1 × 326 g/11½ oz can sweetcorn,	*1 × 11½ oz can kernel corn,*
* drained*	* drained*
salt	*salt*
freshly ground black pepper	*freshly ground black pepper*
vegetable oil for shallow frying	*salad oil for shallow frying*
lemon wedges to serve	*lemon wedges to serve*

Beat the egg yolks and flour together in a bowl. Stir in the corn, and salt and pepper to taste. Beat the egg whites until stiff but not dry and fold into the mixture.

Heat a little oil in a frying pan (skillet). Drop tablespoonfuls of the mixture into the pan, several at a time, and cook for 2 minutes on each side. Remove from the pan with a slotted spoon, drain and keep hot while cooking the remaining mixture. Serve hot with lemon wedges.
Serves 4

Dhal

METRIC/IMPERIAL	AMERICAN
2 tablespoons oil	2 tablespoons oil
2 onions, chopped	2 onions, chopped
½ teaspoon turmeric	½ teaspoon turmeric
¼ teaspoon chilli powder	¼ teaspoon chili powder
225 g/8 oz lentils	1 cup lentils
1 garlic clove, crushed	1 garlic clove, crushed
1 teaspoon sea salt	1 teaspoon coarse salt
750 ml/1¼ pints stock	3 cups stock
3 tomatoes, skinned and chopped	3 tomatoes, skinned and chopped

Heat the oil in a pan, add the onion and fry until softened. Add the turmeric and chilli powder and cook for a further 2 minutes.

Add the remaining ingredients and cook for 50 to 60 minutes, until the lentils are soft. Check the seasoning. Serve with a curry.
Serves 6 to 8

Boston Baked Beans

METRIC/IMPERIAL	AMERICAN
350 g/12 oz haricot beans	1¾ cups navy beans
2 tablespoons olive oil	2 tablespoons olive oil
1 onion, chopped	1 onion, chopped
1 × 226 g/8 oz can tomatoes	1 × ½ lb can tomatoes
pinch of salt	pinch of salt
1 teaspoon dry mustard	1 teaspoon dry mustard
2 teaspoons black treacle	2 teaspoons molasses
1 teaspoon demerara sugar	1 teaspoon light brown sugar
freshly ground black pepper	freshly ground black pepper

Cover the beans with cold water and leave to soak overnight. Drain, rinse well, and drain again. Put in a pan, cover with fresh cold water and bring to the boil. Lower the heat, cover and simmer for 1 hour. Drain, reserving the liquid.

Heat the oil in a frying pan (skillet), add the onion and cook until soft but not browned. Add the beans, tomatoes with their juice, reserved bean water and remaining ingredients, with pepper to taste. Bring to the boil, then transfer to a casserole dish.

Place in a preheated cool oven (150°C/300°F, Gas Mark 2) and cook for 3 hours. Add a little water if the casserole gets too dry.
Serves 4

Gratin Dauphinoise

METRIC/IMPERIAL	AMERICAN
500 g/1 lb potatoes, sliced	1 lb potatoes, sliced
3 garlic cloves, crushed	3 garlic cloves, minced
freshly ground black pepper	freshly ground black pepper
sea salt	coarse salt
300 ml/½ pint single cream	1¼ cups light cream
100 g/4 oz Parmesan cheese, grated	1 cup grated Parmesan cheese

Put one quarter of the potatoes in an ovenproof dish. Cover with one quarter of the garlic, a grinding of pepper, salt to taste, one quarter of the cream and one quarter of the cheese. Repeat the layers 3 more times.

Place in a preheated moderate oven (180°C/350°F, Gas Mark 4) and bake for 1 to 1½ hours until the potatoes are tender.
Serves 4

Potato Latke

METRIC/IMPERIAL	AMERICAN
500 g/1 lb potatoes, grated	1 lb potatoes, grated
225 g/8 oz onions, grated	½ lb onions, grated
2 eggs	2 eggs
salt	salt
freshly ground black pepper	freshly ground black pepper
fat for frying	fat for frying

Mix the ingredients well together, with salt and pepper to taste.

Heat a little fat in a heavy-based frying pan (skillet). Drop in 2 tablespoonfuls of the mixture, flatten with a fish slice and fry for 4 minutes on each side; you can fry about 4 latke at once. Remove from the pan and keep hot while cooking the remainder, adding more fat to the pan as necessary.
Serves 4

SALADS

Waldorf Salad

METRIC/IMPERIAL
2 dessert apples, peeled and sliced
50 g/2 oz walnuts, chopped
2 sticks celery, chopped
2 tablespoons raisins
4 tablespoons mayonnaise (see below)

AMERICAN
2 dessert apples, peeled and sliced
½ cup chopped walnuts
2 celery stalks, chopped
2 tablespoons raisins
¼ cup mayonnaise (see below)

Place the apples, walnuts, celery and raisins in a salad bowl. Stir in the mayonnaise. Chill well before serving.
Serves 4

Mayonnaise

METRIC/IMPERIAL
2 egg yolks
½ teaspoon salt
¼ teaspoon dry mustard
¼ teaspoon freshly ground black pepper
¼ teaspoon sugar
300 ml/½ pint olive oil
1 tablespoon vinegar or lemon juice

AMERICAN
2 egg yolks
½ teaspoon salt
¼ teaspoon dry mustard
¼ teaspoon freshly ground black pepper
¼ teaspoon sugar
1¼ cups olive oil
1 tablespoon vinegar or lemon juice

Make sure that all the ingredients are at room temperature.
Put the egg yolks in a bowl with the seasonings and sugar. Mix thoroughly, then add the oil drop by drop, beating constantly, until the sauce is thick and smooth. Add the vinegar gradually and mix thoroughly.
Makes 300 ml/½ pint/1¼ cups

ORANGE AND ENDIVE (CHICORY) SALAD *(page 74)*;
ASPARAGUS WITH PEAS *(page 66)*

Orange and Endive (Chicory) Salad

METRIC/IMPERIAL
1 head curly endive
1 × 113 g/4 oz can red peppers, drained and sliced
3 small onions, thinly sliced into rings
16 black or green olives, stoned
2 oranges, peeled and thinly sliced into rounds
Dressing:
4 tablespoons olive oil
1 tablespoon wine vinegar
1 garlic clove, crushed
pinch of salt
pinch of sugar
little fresh or dried tarragon

AMERICAN
1 head chicory
1 × ¼ lb can red peppers, drained and sliced
3 small onions, thinly sliced into rings
16 ripe or green olives, pitted
2 oranges, peeled and thinly sliced into rounds
Dressing:
¼ cup olive oil
1 tablespoon wine vinegar
1 garlic clove, crushed
pinch of salt
pinch of sugar
little fresh or dried tarragon

Mix all the salad ingredients together in a salad bowl, preferably wooden. Combine the ingredients for the dressing in a screwtop jar. Shake well and pour over the salad just before serving.
Serves 4

Bean and Tomato Salad

METRIC/IMPERIAL
225 g/8 oz French or runner beans, sliced
salt
225 g/8 oz tomatoes, sliced
1 small onion, chopped
2 tablespoons French dressing (see page 79)
chopped parsley to garnish

AMERICAN
½ lb green beans, sliced
salt
½ lb tomatoes, sliced
1 small onion, chopped
2 tablespoons French dressing (see page 79)
chopped parsley to garnish

Cook the beans in a little boiling salted water until just tender but still crisp. Drain, rinse under cold water, drain well and leave to cool.

Place the beans, tomatoes and onion in a salad bowl. Pour over the dressing and toss well to coat. Chill well. Garnish with chopped parsley to serve.
Serves 4

Brown Rice Salad

METRIC/IMPERIAL
50 g/2 oz brown rice
750 ml/1¼ pints water
salt
2 red peppers, cored, seeded and cut
  into strips
2 tomatoes, diced
3 pineapple rings, chopped
75 g/3 oz blanched, slivered
  almonds, toasted
1 tablespoon chopped parsley
3 tablespoons French dressing (see
  page 79)
1 small lettuce

AMERICAN
¼ cup brown rice
3 cups water
salt
2 red peppers, cored, seeded and cut
  into strips
2 tomatoes, diced
3 pineapple rings, chopped
¾ cup blanched, slivered almonds,
  toasted
1 tablespoon chopped parsley
3 tablespoons French dressing (see
  page 79)
1 head of lettuce

Put the rice in a saucepan with the water and salt. Bring to the boil and boil rapidly for 5 minutes. Cover, lower the heat and cook gently for 40 minutes.

Drain the rice and mix with the red peppers, tomatoes, pineapple and almonds. Stir in the parsley, then pour over the French dressing. Toss well to coat then chill. Serve the rice on a bed of lettuce.
Serves 4

Lentil and Onion Salad

METRIC/IMPERIAL
225 g/8 oz brown lentils
1 teaspoon sea salt
4 tablespoons French dressing
  (see page 79)
1 small green pepper, cored, seeded
  and chopped
1 small onion, finely chopped
2 sticks celery, chopped
1 tablespoon chopped parsley to
- garnish

AMERICAN
1 cup lentils
1 teaspoon coarse salt
¼ cup French dressing
  (see page 79)
1 small green pepper, cored, seeded
  and chopped
1 small onion, finely chopped
2 celery stalks, chopped
1 tablespoon chopped parsley to
  garnish

Place the lentils in a pan, cover with cold water and leave to soak for 1 hour; drain. Cover with fresh cold water, add the salt and bring to the boil. Cook gently for 40 to 45 minutes; drain well. Mix with the dressing while still warm.

Add the pepper, onion and celery and toss together well to coat. Leave to cool. Sprinkle with parsley to serve.
Serves 6

Nut Coleslaw

METRIC/IMPERIAL	AMERICAN
350 g/12 oz white cabbage, shredded	4½ cups finely chopped white cabbage
3 sticks celery, sliced	3 celery stalks, sliced
1 large carrot, grated	1 large carrot, grated
2 red dessert apples, sliced	2 red dessert apples, sliced
juice of ½ lemon	juice of ½ lemon
1 orange, peeled and segmented	1 orange, peeled and segmented
3 spring onions, chopped	3 scallions, chopped
50 g/2 oz walnuts, chopped	½ cup chopped walnuts
25 g/1 oz sultanas	3 tablespoons seedless white raisins
150 ml/¼ pint soured cream	⅔ cup sour cream
2 tablespoons mayonnaise (see page 72)	2 tablespoons mayonnaise (see page 72)
salt	salt
freshly ground black pepper	freshly ground black pepper

Place the cabbage, celery and carrot in a large bowl. Toss the apples in the lemon juice and add to the bowl with the orange, spring onions (scallions), nuts and sultanas (seedless white raisins).

Combine the soured cream and mayonnaise and season to taste with salt and pepper. Add to the cabbage mixture and toss until well coated.

Serves 4

Broad (Lima) Bean Salad

METRIC/IMPERIAL	AMERICAN
225 g/8 oz shelled broad beans	½ lb shelled lima beans
salt	salt
1 onion, chopped	1 onion, chopped
2 tablespoons French dressing (see page 79)	2 tablespoons French dressing (see page 79)
1 tablespoon German mustard	1 tablespoon German mustard
few lettuce leaves	few lettuce leaves

Cook the beans in a little boiling salted water until just tender. Drain well and leave to cool; then mix with the onion.

Combine the French dressing and mustard, pour over the bean mixture and toss well to coat.

Arrange the lettuce in a salad bowl and place the bean mixture on top.

Serves 2

Hot Potato Salad

METRIC/IMPERIAL	AMERICAN
4 tablespoons oil	1/4 cup oil
1 large onion, chopped	1 large onion, chopped
2 tablespoons wholewheat flour	2 tablespoons wholewheat flour
2 teaspoons sugar	2 teaspoons sugar
sea salt	coarse salt
freshly ground black pepper	freshly ground black pepper
150 ml/1/4 pint tarragon vinegar	2/3 cup tarragon vinegar
150 ml/1/4 pint stock	2/3 cup stock
1 kg/2 lb potatoes, boiled and sliced	2 lb potatoes, boiled and sliced
4 spring onions, chopped	4 scallions, chopped
1/2 green pepper, cored, seeded and chopped	1/2 green pepper, cored, seeded and chopped
4 dill pickles, chopped	4 dill pickles, chopped

Heat the oil in a large pan, add the onion and fry until softened. Stir in the flour and cook for 1 minute. Add the sugar, and salt and pepper to taste. Gradually stir in the vinegar and stock. Bring to the boil, stirring, and cook for 2 minutes. Stir in the potatoes, spring onions (scallions), pepper and pickles. The vegetables should be well coated and heated through. Transfer to a salad bowl and serve immediately.
Serves 4 to 6

Mushroom and Spinach Salad

METRIC/IMPERIAL	AMERICAN
100 g/4 oz button mushrooms, thinly sliced	1 cup button mushrooms, thinly sliced
3-4 tablespoons French dressing (see page 79)	3-4 tablespoons French dressing (see page 79)
100 g/4 oz spinach	1/4 lb spinach

Put the mushrooms in a salad bowl with 2 tablespoons of the dressing and stir until well coated. Leave to soak for 1 hour.

Remove the thick centre stalks from the spinach. Wash and drain thoroughly. Slice the leaves finely and mix with the mushrooms, adding more dressing as necessary.
Serves 4

Cauliflower and Nut Salad

METRIC/IMPERIAL
1 cauliflower, divided into florets
salt
50 g/2 oz Danish blue cheese, diced
50 g/2 oz hazelnuts, coarsely
  chopped
1 bunch watercress
2 tablespoons French dressing (see
  below)

AMERICAN
1 cauliflower, broken into florets
salt
½ cup diced blue cheese
½ cup coarsely chopped filberts
1 bunch watercress or American
cress
2 tablespoons French dressing (see
  below)

Cook the cauliflower in boiling salted water until just tender, but still quite crisp. Drain, rinse under cold water, drain well and leave to cool.

Place in a salad bowl with the cheese, nuts and watercress. Pour over the dressing and toss well to coat. Chill well.
Serves 4

French Dressing

METRIC/IMPERIAL
¼ teaspoon salt
pinch of freshly ground black
  pepper
¼ teaspoon dry mustard
¼ teaspoon sugar
1 tablespoon vinegar
3 tablespoons oil

AMERICAN
¼ teaspoon salt
pinch of freshly ground black
  pepper
¼ teaspoon dry mustard
¼ teaspoon sugar
1 tablespoon vinegar
3 tablespoons oil

Put all the ingredients in a screwtop jar and shake well to blend.
Makes 4 tablespoons

Granada Salad

METRIC/IMPERIAL

Omelet:
2 eggs, beaten
1 tablespoon milk
salt
oil for frying

Salad:
1 dessert apple, cored and sliced
1 tablespoon lemon juice
1 red pepper, seeded and cut in
   strips
100 g/4 oz mushrooms, sliced
2 large potatoes, boiled and diced
75 g/3 oz stuffed green olives, sliced
1 head of lettuce

Dressing:
2 tablespoons olive oil
2 tablespoons dry sherry
2 teaspoons Worcestershire sauce
1 teaspoon caster sugar
salt
freshly ground black pepper
25 g/1 oz almonds, chopped

AMERICAN

Omelet:
2 eggs, beaten
1 tablespoon milk
salt
oil for frying

Salad:
1 dessert apple, cored and sliced
1 tablespoon lemon juice
1 red pepper, seeded and cut in
   strips
1 cup sliced mushrooms
2 large potatoes, boiled and diced
1 cup sliced stuffed green olives
1 head of lettuce

Dressing:
2 tablespoons olive oil
2 tablespoons dry sherry
2 teaspoons Worcestershire sauce
1 teaspoon sugar
salt
freshly ground black pepper
¼ cup chopped almonds

Beat together the eggs, milk and salt. Heat the oil in a frying pan (skillet), pour in the egg mixture and cook gently until set. Turn out onto a plate, cool, and cut into squares.

Toss the apple in lemon juice and put aside. Arrange the pepper, mushrooms, potatoes, olives and lettuce in a salad bowl, and place the apple and omelet on top.

Mix together the oil, sherry, Worcester sauce, sugar, seasoning and almonds. Pour over the salad, and toss gently.
Serves 4

GRANADA SALAD
(Photograph: Olives from Spain)

BAKING

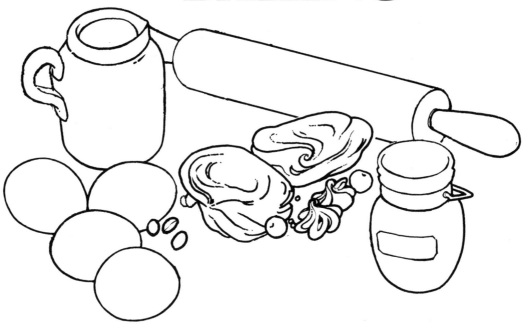

Farmhouse Date Cake

METRIC/IMPERIAL
125 g/5 oz butter or margarine
125 g/5 oz barbados sugar
2 tablespoons black treacle
2 eggs
225 g/8 oz wholewheat flour
2 teaspoons baking powder
1 teaspoon cinnamon
225 g/8 oz stoned dates, chopped
6 tablespoons milk

AMERICAN
2/3 cup butter or margarine
3/4 cup molasses sugar
2 tablespoons molasses
2 eggs
2 cups wholewheat flour
2 teaspoons baking soda
1 teaspoon cinnamon
1 1/2 cups chopped stoned dates
6 tablespoons milk

Cream the fat, sugar and treacle (molasses) together until soft and creamy. Add the eggs one at a time, adding a tablespoon of flour with the second egg. Sift the baking powder (soda) and cinnamon together and fold into the creamed mixture with the remaining flour, the dates and the milk.

Turn into a greased and lined 18 cm/7 inch deep cake tin and bake in a preheated moderate oven (160°C/325°F, Gas Mark 3) for 1 3/4 to 2 hours, or until a skewer inserted into the centre of the cake comes out clean. Turn out onto a wire rack to cool.
Makes one 18 cm/7 inch cake

Banana Cake

METRIC/IMPERIAL	AMERICAN
100 g/4 oz margarine	½ cup margarine
100 g/4 oz soft brown sugar	⅔ cup soft brown sugar
2 eggs	2 eggs
125 g/5 oz wholewheat flour	1 ¼ cups wholewheat flour
2 teaspoons baking powder	2 teaspoons baking soda
2 bananas, mashed	2 bananas, mashed
1 tablespoon finely chopped walnuts	1 tablespoon finely chopped walnuts

Cream the fat and the sugar together until light and fluffy. Add the eggs one at a time, adding a tablespoon of flour with the second egg. Fold in the remaining flour and sift in the baking powder (soda); then carefully fold in the bananas. Turn into a greased and lined 18 cm/7 inch deep cake tin and sprinkle the walnuts over the top.

Bake in a preheated moderate oven (180°C/350°F, Gas Mark 4) for 1 hour or until a skewer inserted into the centre of the cake comes out clean. Turn on to a wire rack to cool.

Makes one 18 cm/7 inch cake

Walnut Flapjacks

METRIC/IMPERIAL	AMERICAN
100 g/4 oz margarine	½ cup margarine
100 g/4 oz demerara sugar	⅔ cup light brown sugar
4 tablespoons golden syrup	¼ cup light corn syrup
225 g/8 oz rolled oats	2 ¼ cups rolled oats
50 g/2 oz walnuts, chopped finely	½ cup finely chopped walnuts

Melt the margarine with the sugar and syrup in a saucepan. Cool slightly; mix in the rolled oats and nuts, and stir thoroughly. Turn into a greased 18 x 28 cm/7 x 11 inch shallow tin. Smooth the top with a palette knife and bake in a preheated moderate oven (180°C/350°F, Gas Mark 4) for 25 to 30 minutes.

Cool in the tin for 2 minutes, then cut into bars. Allow to cool before removing from the tin.

Makes 20

Farmhouse Bread

METRIC/IMPERIAL	AMERICAN
1.5 kg/3 lb wholewheat bread flour	12 cups wholewheat flour
1 tablespoon sea salt	1 tablespoon coarse salt
25 g/1 oz Muscovado sugar	1½ tablespoons Barbados sugar
25 g/1 oz fresh yeast	1 cake compressed yeast
900 ml/1½ pints lukewarm water	3¾ cups lukewarm water
1 tablespoon vegetable oil	1 tablespoon vegetable oil
beaten egg to glaze	beaten egg to glaze

Put the flour, salt and sugar in a warm bowl and mix well. Blend the yeast with a little of the water, then stir into the remaining water and add to the dry ingredients with the oil. Mix to a soft dough.

Turn out onto a lightly floured surface and knead for 5 minutes until smooth. Place in a warm, greased bowl, cover with a damp cloth and leave in a warm place for about 1 hour until doubled in size.

Turn out onto the floured surface and knead again for 5 minutes, then divide into 4 pieces. Fold each piece into 3, then place in greased warmed 500 g/1 lb/8 x 4½ x 2½ inch loaf pans. Cover with a damp cloth and leave in a warm place for about 30 minutes until the dough rises to the tops of the pans.

Brush with beaten egg, place in a preheated hot oven (220°C/425°F, Gas Mark 7) and bake for 40 minutes. Turn out onto a wire rack to cool.
Makes four 500 g/1 lb loaves

Wholewheat Baps

Make as for Farmhouse Bread above but divide the dough into 24 pieces and shape into round flat baps (buns). Place on greased, warmed baking (cookie) sheets and sprinkle with a little wholewheat flour. Cover with a damp cloth and leave to rise in a warm place until doubled in size.

Bake in a preheated hot oven (220°C/425°F, Gas Mark 7) for 15 minutes. Remove and wrap immediately in a clean cloth; this will keep them soft, by trapping the steam as they cool.
Makes 24

FARMHOUSE BREAD; WHOLEWHEAT BAPS
FRUIT MALT LOAF *(page 86)*; BRAN BREAD *(page 87)*

Fruit Malt Loaf

METRIC/IMPERIAL	AMERICAN
225 g/8 oz wholewheat flour	*2 cups wholewheat flour*
¼ teaspoon sea salt	*¼ teaspoon coarse salt*
100 g/4 oz sultanas	*¾ cup seedless white raisins*
25 g/1 oz margarine	*2 tablespoons margarine*
50 g/2 oz malt extract	*3 tablespoons malt extract*
25 g/1 oz black treacle	*1½ tablespoons molasses*
15 g/½ oz fresh yeast	*½ cake compressed yeast*
5 tablespoons lukewarm water	*⅔ cup lukewarm water*
1 tablespoon clear honey to glaze	*1 tablespoon clear honey to glaze*

Put the flour, salt and sultanas (seedless white raisins) in a warm bowl and mix well. Put the margarine, malt extract and black treacle (molasses) in a pan and heat gently until the margarine has melted. Leave to cool for 5 minutes.

Blend the yeast with the water, then add to the dry ingredients with the melted mixture. Mix to a soft dough.

Turn out onto a lightly floured surface and knead for 5 minutes until smooth. Place the dough in a warmed greased bowl. Cover and leave in a warm place for about 2 to 3 hours until doubled in size.

Turn out onto the floured surface and knead again for 5 minutes. Fold the dough into 3, then place in a greased, warmed 500 g/1 lb/ 8 x 4½ x 2½ inch loaf pan. Cover with a clean damp cloth and leave in a warm place for about 1 hour until the dough rises to the top of the pan. Place in a preheated moderately hot oven (190°C/375°F, Gas Mark 5) for 45 minutes. Turn out onto a wire rack, brush with honey, and leave to cool.

Makes one 500 g/1 lb loaf

Bran Bread

METRIC/IMPERIAL
600 g/1 ¼ lb wholewheat bread
  flour
100 g/4 oz bran
15 g/½ oz sea salt
25 g/1 oz Muscovado sugar
25 g/1 oz fresh yeast
450 ml/¾ pint lukewarm water
1 tablespoon oil
To finish:
2 tablespoons cold water
pinch of salt
2 tablespoons rolled oats

AMERICAN
5 cups wholewheat flour
2 cups bran
1½ teaspoons coarse salt
1½ tablespoons Barbados sugar
1 cake compressed yeast
2 cups lukewarm water
1 tablespoon oil
To finish:
2 tablespoons cold water
pinch of salt
2 tablespoons rolled oats

Put the flour, bran, salt and sugar in a warm bowl and mix well. Blend the yeast with a little of the water, then stir into the remaining water and add to the dry ingredients with the oil. Mix to a firm dough.

Turn out onto a lightly floured surface and knead for 5 minutes until smooth. Place in a warm, greased bowl, cover with a damp cloth and leave in a warm place for about 1 hour until doubled in size.

Turn out onto the floured surface and knead again for 5 minutes, then divide in half. Shape each piece of dough and place in greased, warmed 500 g/1 lb/8 x 4½ x 2½ inch loaf pans. Cover with a damp cloth and leave in a warm place for about 30 minutes until the dough rises to the tops of the pans.

Mix the cold water and salt together, brush over the tops of the loaves and sprinkle with the oats. Place in a preheated hot oven (220°C/425°F, Gas Mark 7) and bake for 35 to 40 minutes until well risen and crisp. Turn out onto a wire rack to cool.

Makes two 500 g/1 lb loaves

Cottage Cheese Griddle Cakes

METRIC/IMPERIAL
25 g/1 oz margarine, melted
100 g/4 oz cottage cheese
2 eggs, beaten
50 g/2 oz wholewheat flour
1 teaspoon baking powder
1 tablespoon milk

AMERICAN
2 tablespoons margarine, melted
½ cup cottage cheese
2 eggs, beaten
½ cup wholewheat flour
1 teaspoon baking powder
1 tablespoon milk

Put the margarine and cheese in a bowl and mix well. Beat in the eggs, then stir in the flour, baking powder and milk and beat to a smooth thick batter.

Grease a griddle or heavy-based frying pan (skillet) very lightly with fat and heat until very hot.

Drop tablespoonfuls of the batter onto the hot surface. Cook for 1 minute until just set, then turn over and cook for a further 1 minute. Turn over again and continue cooking until the griddle cakes are set and golden in colour.

Transfer to a wire rack and cover with a clean cloth to keep hot while cooking the remaining batter. Serve hot with honey or a savoury spread.

Makes 10 to 12 griddle cakes

Yogurt Wholewheat Scones

METRIC/IMPERIAL
225 g/8 oz wholewheat flour
½ teaspoon salt
1½ teaspoons baking powder
50 g/2 oz margarine
1 x 141 g/5 oz carton natural
  yogurt

AMERICAN
2 cups wholewheat flour
½ teaspoon salt
1½ teaspoons baking powder
¼ cup margarine
⅔ cup unflavored yogurt

Put the flour, salt and baking powder in a bowl and mix well. Rub in the margarine, then stir in the yogurt and mix to a soft dough.

Turn out on to a lightly floured surface and knead lightly for 30 seconds. Roll out to 2 cm/¾ inch thickness, cut out 10 rounds with a 5 cm/2 inch cutter and place on a greased baking (cookie) sheet.

Place in a preheated moderately hot oven (200°C/400°F, Gas Mark 6) and bake for 12 minutes. Transfer to a wire rack to cool. Serve with honey or a cheese spread.

Makes 10 scones

Wholewheat Soda Bread

METRIC/IMPERIAL
350 g/12 oz wholewheat flour
100 g/4 oz plain flour
1 teaspoon salt
1 teaspoon bicarbonate of soda
25 g/1 oz lard
300 ml/½ pint buttermilk

AMERICAN
3 cups wholewheat flour
1 cup all-purpose flour
1 teaspoon salt
1 teaspoon baking soda
2 tablespoons shortening
1¼ cups buttermilk

Sift the dry ingredients into a bowl. Cut in the fat and rub in until the mixture resembles breadcrumbs. Stir in the buttermilk and work until the mixture draws together, then knead well. Turn on to a lightly floured surface, and shape into an 18 cm/7 inch round.

Place on a greased baking (cookie) sheet and mark into quarters with a sharp knife. Place in a preheated moderately hot oven (200°C/400°F, Gas Mark 6) and bake for about 35 minutes, until risen and golden. Cool on a wire rack. Serve the same day.
Makes one 18 cm/7 inch round loaf

Cheese and Nut Loaf

METRIC/IMPERIAL
225 g/8 oz wholewheat flour
2 teaspoons baking powder
1 teaspoon dry mustard powder
1 teaspoon salt
freshly ground black pepper
75 g/3 oz butter
100 g/4 oz Cheddar cheese, grated
25 g/1 oz salted peanuts, chopped
2 large eggs
150 ml/¼ pint milk

AMERICAN
2 cups wholewheat flour
2 teaspoons baking powder
1 teaspoon dry mustard powder
1 teaspoon salt
freshly ground black pepper
⅓ cup butter
1 cup grated Cheddar cheese
¼ cup chopped salted peanuts
2 large eggs
⅔ cup milk

Sift the dry ingredients, with pepper to taste, into a bowl. Rub in the butter until the mixture resembles breadcrumbs. Stir in the cheese and nuts. Beat together the eggs and milk and mix into the dry ingredients to make a stiff dough.

Turn into a greased 500 g/1 lb/8 x 4½ x 2½ inch loaf tin and bake in a preheated moderate oven (180°C/350°F, Gas Mark 4) for 1 hour. Turn out onto a wire rack to cool. Cut into slices to serve.
Makes one 500 g/1 lb loaf

INDEX

INDEX

PDO 80-59